From the Host of the
Snowbirds Expat Radio Podcas

THE GREAT RETURN: CANADIANS GUIDE TO MOVING HOME FROM THE US

Taxes, Residency, Healthcare and the Mistakes Returning Canadians make

Gerald A Scott

Table of Contents

DISCLAIMER

This book is written by Gerry A. Scott in their individual capacity and not as a registered representation of Raymond James Ltd. (RJL) or any of its affiliates. It expresses the opinions of the authors and not necessarily those of RJL or any of its affiliates. This book is provided as a general source of information and should not be considered personal investment advice or financial planning advice. It should not be construed as an offer or solicitation for the sale or purchase of any product and should not be considered tax advice. We are not tax advisors and we recommend that clients seek independent advice from a professional advisor on tax-related matters. We recommend any individual seek independent advice from an investment advisor prior to making any investment decisions and from a professional accountant concerning tax-related matters. Statistics, factual data and other information are from sources RJL believes to be reliable, but their accuracy cannot be guaranteed. This book is furnished on the basis and understanding that RJL or any of its affiliates are to be under no liability whatsoever in respect therefore. This book may provide reference to third-party services. RJL or any of its affiliates is not responsible for the availability of these external services, nor does RJL or any of its affiliates endorse, warrant or guarantee the products, services or information described or offered. US-based securities-related products and services are offered through Raymond James (USA) Ltd., member FINRA/SIPC.

This book is intended for informational and educational purposes only. It is based on general principles and analysis of cross-border tax, residency, and regulatory frameworks as understood at the time of writing. It does not constitute legal, tax, investment, financial, immigration, or estate-planning advice, and should not be relied upon as such.

The information contained herein reflects general principles and observations at the time of writing. Laws, regulations, tax rules, and administrative practices in both Canada and the United States are complex and subject to change. Individual circumstances vary widely, and readers should always consult their own qualified professional advisors before making any decisions based on the content of this book.

Any examples, case studies, or scenarios described are illustrative only and are not intended to represent any specific individual or outcome. Past experiences or outcomes discussed do not guarantee future results.

Neither the author nor any affiliated organizations assume responsibility for errors, omissions, or for actions taken by readers based on the information contained in this book.

WHY THIS BOOK EXISTS

I've been travelling between Canada and the United States for most of my adult life—from my first visit to Maui in 1980, to obtaining an E-2 visa, incorporating our apps and podcast, and working across both countries, legally.

Along the way, I've met—and worked with—many Canadians navigating life on both sides of the border.

In our first book, we focused on snowbirds heading south and the hidden risks they face—what you don't know can hurt you.

This second book is different. It's for Canadians coming home.

After decades living and working in the United States, many assume returning to Canada will be simple. It's not. The cross-border landscape is complex, and the consequences of getting it wrong can be significant—from tax exposure and residency issues to healthcare access and financial planning missteps.

As a cross-border portfolio manager licensed in both countries, I've seen these challenges firsthand. Our wealth management practice is built around helping clients navigate exactly these situations.

We've also seen a growing trend: more Canadians returning home, and more Americans looking north for new opportunities. Immigration lawyers, cross-border tax specialists, and financial professionals are busier than ever—many are no longer accepting new clients.

Regardless of the reasons behind this movement, one thing is clear:

It's happening.

And people need help.

This book is designed to provide that guidance—to help you understand the risks, avoid costly mistakes, and connect with the right professionals when needed. Many of the insights shared here are drawn from real-world experience and conversations featured on the Snowbirds Expat Radio Podcast.

These are not theories. These are lived experiences.

Looking ahead, there may be a third book—focused on Canadians seeking to move south. Time will tell. These projects take time, care, and a genuine commitment to getting it right.

At the core of everything we do is a simple belief: Helping people matters.

I was raised with that mindset, and it continues to guide both my work and this book. While we are fortunate to be well-compensated for what we do, the real reward comes from helping people navigate important life transitions with confidence and clarity.

That's why this book exists.

HOW TO READ THIS BOOK

This book is designed to be practical, clear, and easy to navigate—much like our first book for snowbirds heading south.

You don't need to read it cover to cover in one sitting.

Each chapter focuses on a specific area of the cross-border journey—tax, residency, healthcare, financial planning, and more—so you can go directly to the sections most relevant to your situation.

If you're early in the process, we recommend starting from the beginning to build a strong foundation. If you're further along, feel free to jump to the chapters that address your immediate concerns.

Throughout the book, you'll find real-world examples and case studies drawn from our day-to-day experience working with clients in the Canada–U.S. cross-border space.

Use this book as a guide, a reference, and a starting point for conversations with the right professionals.

Because when it comes to cross-border planning, informed decisions make all the difference.

A NOTE OF GRATITUDE

We are incredibly grateful for the many clients, listeners, and professionals who have trusted us over the years.

To those who have shared their stories, experiences, and challenges—thank you. Your journeys have helped shape the insights found in this book.

We also extend our appreciation to the cross-border professionals—tax specialists, immigration lawyers, and advisors—who continue to do important work in an increasingly complex environment.

And to our families and team, thank you for your continued support. These projects take time, energy, and commitment, and none of this would be possible without you.

We feel fortunate to do what we do.

Helping people navigate these transitions is a responsibility we take seriously—and a privilege we never take for granted.

INTRODUCTION

This book is for Canadians who are making their way home after years of living or working in the United States.

For many people, that decision carries a natural sense of relief. Home is familiar. The direction feels clear. What is often less clear is what the return actually sets in motion once it begins.

Coming back to Canada is not only a personal move. It is also a transition through systems that do not always respond at the same pace or in the same way. Questions that seemed distant while living in the United States can become immediate once the return becomes real. Timing matters. Sequence matters. So does understanding which parts of life need to be revisited first and which assumptions no longer hold once you are re-establishing yourself in Canada.

HOW I CAME TO THIS WORK

I did not begin my career expecting to focus on Canadians returning home after years of living or working in the United States. Like many professional paths, mine developed over time through experience, client needs, and years of seeing where important decisions begin to collide.

I grew up in a working family where effort, responsibility, and attention to detail were simply part of daily life. Those values stayed with me. When I later moved into financial services, I became increasingly interested in how people's financial lives evolve over time, especially when major life transitions force earlier decisions to be revisited.

Over the years, that work kept leading me toward more complex situations. I began seeing how often Canadians returning from the United States faced problems they had not anticipated while living there. They were not looking for abstract explanations. They wanted to understand what their return would affect, what had to be handled first, and what mistakes were most likely to create lasting consequences.

I have now spent 35 years as an advisor, and the last 10 years as a cross-border advisor. That work has shown me how often a return to Canada brings practical issues into focus only after the process has already begun.

This book grows out of that experience and out of the many conversations I have had with Canadians trying to come home with clarity, protect what they built, and move into the next stage of life without unnecessary complications.

CASE STUDIES THROUGHOUT

Throughout this book, you will find case studies based on real situations faced by Canadians returning home after years of living or working in the United States. These examples are included to show how cross-border issues unfold in practice — how assumptions are made, where timing goes wrong, and how clearer planning could have improved the outcome.

Their purpose is not to dramatize the process, but to make it easier to understand.

PODCAST DISCUSSIONS

The Snowbirds Expat Radio Podcast has been an important part of the cross-border conversations that shaped this book. Through listener questions, professional interviews, and practical discussions, the podcast has helped surface the issues people most often misunderstand when returning to Canada.

These discussions have been especially valuable because they reflect what people are actually asking, worrying about, and trying to solve as they prepare to come home.

TRACKING APP

The tracking app is another practical tool that supports this process. For people navigating cross-border movement, accurate records matter. Dates, presence patterns, and timing can all influence how different systems interpret a return.

A tracking tool helps reduce guesswork and provides a clearer record of movement, which can be important when residency, eligibility, or reporting questions arise.

PLANNING TOOLS AND REFERENCE MATERIALS

This book also draws on broader planning tools and reference materials developed through years of cross-border work. These are meant to help readers identify key decision points and approach the return to Canada in a more organized way.

They are not a substitute for professional advice. They are meant to help readers prepare more deliberately.

CHAPTER 1
COVERED EXPATRIATE OR NON-COVERED EXPATRIATE?

THE QUESTION THAT STOPS CANADIANS IN THEIR TRACKS

We were only weeks away from production on *The Great Canadian Return* when it became clear that one issue had to come first.

Not later in the book. Not buried inside a broader tax discussion. Not treated as a side note.

It had to be Chapter 1.

Because for many Canadians leaving the United States and moving back to Canada, nothing matters more at the outset than this question:

Am I a covered expatriate or a non-covered expatriate?

That single question can stop the entire move in its tracks.

You can plan the sale of the house. You can organize your shipment, say goodbye to friends, and start picturing your next chapter back home.

But if you are surrendering a green card after being a long-term

U.S. resident—or renouncing U.S. citizenship—you may be stepping into one of the most important tax events of your life.

And many people do not see it coming.

WHY THIS MATTERS SO MUCH

Many Canadians who moved to the United States years ago built successful lives there. They may own a home, hold investment accounts, have retirement plans, own interests in private businesses, or simply have experienced decades of market growth and real estate appreciation.

On paper, they may not think of themselves as wealthy.

But the U.S. expatriation rules are not concerned with how "rich" someone feels. They look at specific thresholds and definitions—and importantly, they look at worldwide assets.

And this is where people get caught.

CASE STUDY

BOB AND JUDY: WHEN A SIMPLE MOVE HOME ISN'T SO SIMPLE

Bob and Judy always assumed moving back to Canada would be easy.

They left Ontario in their early 30s, built a life in Arizona, raised their family, and enjoyed a successful run in the United States.

Bob owned a small manufacturing business that he eventually sold. Judy worked in healthcare.

Now in their early 60s, they were ready to come home. They were not U.S. citizens, but they were long-term green card holders, which made the expatriation rules especially important if they chose to formally give up their green cards.

They had a plan:

- Sell their home in Arizona
- Simplify their investments
- Surrender their green cards
- Move back to British Columbia

Straightforward. Clean. Exciting.

Until one question came up:

"Have you looked at whether you're covered expatriates?"

They hadn't.

THEIR BALANCE SHEET TOLD A DIFFERENT STORY

Here's what their situation looked like (USD):

- Arizona home: $1.8 million
- Investment portfolio: $1.6 million

- Retirement accounts: $1.4 million
- Cash and other assets: $200,000

Total net worth: $5 million

Bob's initial reaction was common:

"We're at $5 million combined—we should be fine." But that's not how the rule works.

The $2 million threshold applies per individual, not per couple. When their assets were split:

- Bob: ~$2.7 million
- Judy: ~$2.3 million

Both were over the threshold.

If they surrendered their long-term green cards without planning, both could become covered expatriates because each appeared to meet the net-worth test. The threshold alone did not create the status; the risk arose because they were long-term green card holders considering expatriation.

THE HIDDEN TAX PROBLEM

Bob had sold his business years earlier and reinvested the proceeds. Their portfolio had grown significantly. Their home had appreciated over decades.

They hadn't sold anything recently.

But under U.S. rules, that didn't matter.

If they proceeded as covered expatriates, many of their assets would be treated as if sold the day before expatriation.

They could owe tax on gains they had never realized. That stopped them cold.

Judy said it best:

"Why would we leave if we're going to write a cheque like that?"

WHAT IS A COVERED EXPATRIATE?

Covered expatriate status generally matters when:

- U.S. citizens who renounce citizenship
- Long-term green card holders who formally give up their green cards, generally after holding green card status for 8 of the last 15 years

This is where many Canadians are caught off guard. You do not need to be a U.S. citizen to trigger these rules. Giving up a long-term green card can be enough.

Under U.S. tax rules, you may be classified as a covered expatriate if you give up U.S. citizenship or formally give up a long-term green card and meet any one of the following tests:

1. Net Worth Test

Your net worth is $2 million USD or more on the date of expatriation.

2. Tax Liability Test

Your average annual U.S. income tax liability over the past five years exceeds a specified threshold.

3. Tax Compliance Test

You cannot certify that you have fully complied with U.S. tax obligations for the previous five years.

Simply giving up a green card can be enough.

WHAT IS THE EXIT TAX?

If you are a covered expatriate, the U.S. may apply a mark-to-market tax.

In simple terms:

The IRS treats many of your assets as if they were sold the day before you leave.

Even if you didn't actually sell anything. This includes:

- Investment portfolios
- Real estate (in many cases)
- Business interests
- Other appreciated assets

There is an exemption amount, but anything above that may be taxable.

And certain assets—like retirement accounts—have their own rules.

WHY PEOPLE FREEZE WHEN THEY LEARN THIS

Bob and Judy didn't cancel their move.

But they paused.

Because now the questions changed:

- Should we leave this year or next?
- Should we sell assets before expatriation?
- Should we restructure anything first?
- Are our tax filings fully compliant?
- Should one spouse act before the other?

This is where planning matters.

Because once you trigger expatriation, your options are limited.

WHAT BOB AND JUDY DID NEXT

Instead of moving forward blindly, they:

- Reviewed their last five years of tax filings
- Confirmed their exposure under all three tests
- Analyzed unrealized gains
- Evaluated timing and sequencing
- Worked with cross-border professionals
- Built a structured exit plan, including reviewing whether assets could be reorganized or gifted in advance to reduce individual net worth below the $2 million threshold where appropriate

The move didn't stop.

It became intentional.

THE REAL FIRST STEP

The first step is not booking the move.

It's not selling the house.

It's not even deciding where in Canada you want to live. The first step is this:

Determine whether you may become a covered expatriate before you give up your green card or renounce U.S. citizenship.That means understanding:

- Your net worth
- Your tax history
- Your exposure to unrealized gains
- Your residency timeline
- Your filing compliance
- Whether you qualify as a long-term green card holder under the 8-of-15-year rule

Whether any IRS exceptions to covered expatriate status may apply, especially for certain U.S. citizens, such as dual citizens at birth or individuals who renounce before age 18½

FINAL THOUGHT

For Canadians returning home, there are many moving parts—tax, healthcare, pensions, and planning.

But for those leaving the United States, this issue comes first for a reason.

It can stop you in your tracks. It can reshape your timeline.

And it can significantly impact your wealth.

Bob said it best:

"We thought moving home was the decision.

Turns out, the real decision was how to leave properly." Before you make the move, know where you stand: covered expatriate or non-covered expatriate.

Because when it comes to leaving the United States— what you don't know will hurt you.

LOOKING AHEAD TO CHAPTER 2

Now that you understand one of the most critical decisions when leaving the United States—whether you are a covered expatriate or a non-covered expatriate—you're in a position to move forward with clarity.

But leaving the U.S. is only half the story.

Because for Canadians heading home, the next phase can be just as complex—and in many cases, just as costly if handled incorrectly.

In Chapter 2, we shift our focus to what happens next:

Moving back to Canada and the hidden tax traps every returning Canadian needs to know.

From how your assets are treated when you re-establish Canadian residency, to the risks of double taxation, to the timing decisions that can impact your long-term financial outcome—this is where many well-intentioned plans begin to unravel.

If Chapter 1 was about leaving properly, Chapter 2 is about arriving intelligently.

Because once again—what you don't know will hurt you.

CHAPTER 2
MOVING BACK TO CANADA: THE HIDDEN TAX TRAPS RETURNING CANADIANS NEED TO KNOW

In this chapter, you will learn:

- Why returning to Canada does not automatically end
- U.S. tax obligations
- How and when Canadian tax residency is re-established under CRA rules
- The most common tax and reporting traps faced in the first year back
- How TFSA, RRSP, and retirement account rules change upon return
- What happens to U.S. retirement plans, pensions, and Social Security in Canada
- Why healthcare coverage gaps frequently occur during the transition
- How foreign reporting requirements, including T1135, catch returnees off guard
- Which U.S. obligations continue after departure—and for how long

This chapter provides the technical roadmap needed to return home cleanly, confidently, and without costly surprises.

INTRODUCTION — RETURNING HOME IS NOT A RESET BUTTON

For many Canadians who have spent years building careers, raising families, or enjoying retirement in the United States, moving back to Canada feels like a natural homecoming. Emotionally, it often feels like a return to familiar ground.

From a tax perspective, however, returning home is not a reset.

Canada and the United States operate on different tax systems, different timelines, and different definitions of residency. These systems do not automatically synchronize when you cross the border. As a result, many returning Canadians discover—often too late—that actions they assumed were harmless triggered unexpected tax obligations, penalties, or filing requirements.

This chapter focuses on the most common tax traps Canadians encounter when returning home and explains how those traps arise.

Because a return to Canada may feel familiar.

But from a tax perspective, it is a transition that has to be handled properly.

THE INVISIBLE DEPARTURE TRAP — YOU NEVER OFFICIALLY "LEAVE" THE U.S.

One of the most dangerous assumptions returning Canadians make is believing that the U.S. tax system automatically knows when they have left.

It does not.

Unlike Canada, the United States does not have a formal "departure" process for individuals who stop living there. There is no exit interview, no departure declaration, and no government form that confirms you are no longer part of the U.S. tax system. For the IRS, absence alone does not equal closure.

This creates what I call the invisible departure trap.

People assume that selling a home, closing a U.S. bank account, or physically moving north is enough to end their U.S. tax obligations. In reality, the IRS continues to rely on filings, not assumptions, to determine whether your U.S. tax relationship has ended.

If the paperwork is not handled correctly, the IRS may continue to treat you as if nothing changed.

WHY THE IRS DOESN'T KNOW YOU LEFT

The U.S. tax system is filing-based. The IRS determines your status by what you submit, not by where you live or how convincingly your life appears to have moved on.

If you previously filed U.S. tax returns as a resident, or if you met the Substantial Presence Test in past years, the IRS expects continuity unless you clearly signal a change. Without that signal, the system often assumes residency continues.

This is especially true in the year you leave.

That year frequently requires:

- A final U.S. return or a dual-status return
- Proper reporting of departure timing
- Correct classification of income before and after departure

If this is missed or done incorrectly, the IRS may continue to expect future filings.

A REAL STORY: THE RETIRED NURSE WHO NEVER REALLY LEFT THE U.S. SYSTEM

A retired nurse from British Columbia returned to Canada after ten years in Arizona. She had lived in the United States on a work visa, but she had never become a U.S. citizen and had never obtained a green card.When she returned to Canada, she sold her home, closed local accounts, and believed her U.S. tax obligations had ended.

Two years later, an IRS notice arrived.

The issue was not that she remained a U.S. person. She did not. The problem was that her final U.S. filings had not clearly reflected the end of her U.S. tax residency, and U.S.-source income had continued to be reported to the IRS on tax slips issued in her name. From the IRS's perspective, there was still an open filing issue.

What followed was three years of correspondence, multiple professionals, and thousands of dollars in avoidable costs. The issue was not fraud or evasion. It was an incomplete departure trail.

THE CORE PROBLEM

Leaving the United States does not automatically end your U.S. tax relationship.

If your departure is not reflected properly in your filings, the IRS may continue to treat you as part of the system. And once time passes, correcting that becomes more expensive and more difficult.

WHY THIS SECTION MATTERS

This invisible departure trap often affects everything that follows in the return year. Departure timing, residency overlap, and filing obligations can all become harder to manage when this first step is missed.

CRA RESIDENCY — YOU BECOME A CANADIAN RESIDENT LONG BEFORE YOU EXPECT

Many returning Canadians assume that Canadian tax residency resumes on a clear, obvious date. They expect it to begin when they buy a home, start a job, or physically settle back into daily life. In practice, residency often begins much earlier.

Canada does not use a day-count test to restore tax residency. Instead, the CRA applies a residential ties analysis, which focuses on where your life is centered rather than how many days you are present. This difference between expectation and reality is one of the most common sources of surprise for returning Canadians.

The critical mistake is believing that residency is something you choose or declare. In Canada, residency is inferred from your actions.

HOW CRA DETERMINES YOU ARE A RESIDENT AGAIN

CRA looks at the totality of your circumstances. Certain actions strongly signal that you have resumed life in Canada, even if you believe the return is still temporary.

You are likely considered a Canadian resident once you:

Move into a home in Canada, whether owned or rented

- Bring your spouse or dependents back

- Reactivate provincial health coverage
- Reopen or meaningfully use Canadian banking and investment accounts
- Return with the intention to settle, even if housing or employment is not finalized

No single factor is decisive on its own. What matters is the overall picture. Once those ties reattach, residency can restart quickly.

WHY RESIDENCY OFTEN STARTS EARLIER THAN EXPECTED

From the CRA's perspective, residency begins when Canada becomes the place where your personal and economic life is re-established. The return does not need to be permanent, fully organized, or complete. Even a transitional period can trigger residency if it looks settled in substance.

This is why staying with family, storing personal belongings, or reactivating services can matter more than people realize. These actions indicate continuity and intention, not just presence.

A REAL STORY: THE ENGINEER WHO BECAME A RESIDENT TOO SOON

A Vancouver-born engineer returned from California and stayed with family while searching for a home. He believed Canadian tax residency would begin only after he purchased property.

CRA disagreed.

Because he had already reactivated provincial services, moved personal items back, and was living in Canada with no defined end date, CRA determined that his residency had resumed months earlier. As a result, he owed Canadian tax on worldwide income earned during that period, income he had not expected to report.

The issue was not timing alone. It was interpretation.

WHY THIS CREATES OVERLAPPING TAX RISK

When Canadian residency resumes earlier than expected, it can overlap with ongoing U.S. tax obligations. This overlap often creates:

- Unexpected Canadian tax on U.S.-source income
- Filing complexity in both countries
- Missed planning opportunities around departure timing
- Increased risk of penalties due to misaligned reporting

Once residency is established, Canada expects full disclosure of worldwide income, regardless of where it was earned or paid.

KEY TAKEAWAY

If your return to Canada looks settled in substance, CRA may treat it as settled in law.

Understanding when Canadian residency resumes is not a technical detail. It is the foundation upon which every other tax, reporting, and planning decision in your return year depends.

TFSA ELIGIBILITY — THE UNEXPECTED PENALTY MINEFIELD

For many returning Canadians, the TFSA feels like a familiar and harmless account. That familiarity is exactly what makes it dangerous in the year of return.

While living in the United States as a non-resident of Canada, your TFSA does not accumulate new contribution room for years in which you are non-resident for the entire year. More importantly, contributions made while you are a non-resident can trigger a 1% monthly tax, even if you still have unused TFSA room from earlier years. Once Canadian tax residency is re-established, you may be able to contribute again, but only up to your available TFSA room.

This timing gap catches people off guard.

HOW TFSA CONTRIBUTION RULES ACTUALLY WORK

The TFSA is residency-sensitive. The rules operate on a yearly basis and do not prorate for partial years of residency.

Here is what matters:

- While you are a non-resident of Canada for an entire year, you do not earn new TFSA contribution room for that year.
- Contributions made while you are a non-resident can trigger a 1% monthly tax for as long as the non-resident contribution remains in the account.
- Once you become a Canadian tax resident again, you can generally contribute up to your available TFSA room, which may include unused room from before you left Canada and any current-year room available after residency is restored.
- You do not automatically need to wait until January 1 of the following year, but you do need to verify your room before contributing.

This means the issue is not simply whether you are "back." The issue is whether you were a Canadian tax resident when the contribution was made and whether you had available contribution room at that time.

WHY THE PENALTIES ARE SO SEVERE

CRA enforces TFSA contribution limits aggressively. Excess contributions and non-resident contributions are subject to a 1% penalty per month on the excess amount, and that penalty continues until the overcontribution is corrected.

There is no grace period based on misunderstanding. The rules apply whether the mistake was intentional or accidental.

A REAL STORY: THE EXCESS CONTRIBUTION PENALTY

A woman returning to Alberta after twelve years in Florida assumed she could contribute for every year she had been away.

She could not.

CRA assessed her a 1% monthly penalty on nearly $30,000 in excess contributions. By the time the issue was discovered, the penalties had accumulated for months. The financial cost was painful, but the administrative process of correcting the error was worse.

The mistake was not aggressive planning. It was assuming the TFSA worked the way it always had.

WHY THIS HAPPENS SO OFTEN

TFSA rules feel intuitive when you have always lived in Canada.

Once residency is interrupted, that intuition stops working.

Returning Canadians often:

- Reactivate accounts automatically
- Receive well-meaning advice from friends or institutions
- Assume "being back" means "being eligible"

These assumptions may not align with how the CRA applies TFSA rules.

WHAT RETURNING CANADIANS SHOULD DO INSTEAD

Before contributing to a TFSA after returning to Canada, you must confirm:

- Your exact Canadian residency start date
- Your unused TFSA room from before leaving Canada
- Whether you have current-year TFSA room available after residency is restored
- Whether any withdrawals made before or during non-residency affect future room
- Whether you are still a U.S. citizen or green card holder, because TFSA income may still be taxable on a U.S. tax return

In many cases, the safest approach is to wait until your TFSA room has been confirmed through CRA records or a qualified cross-border tax professional.

KEY TAKEAWAY

The TFSA is one of the most valuable tools available to Canadians. It is also one of the easiest ways for returning residents to trigger avoidable penalties.

Understanding when contribution room actually resumes is essential. Guessing is expensive.

U.S. RETIREMENT PLANS — HOW CANADA TAXES YOUR IRA, 401(K), AND SOCIAL SECURITY

One of the most costly surprises for returning Canadians involves U.S. retirement accounts. Many people assume that because these plans were built under U.S. rules, they will continue to be treated the same way after moving back to Canada.

They are not.

Canada and the United States tax retirement income very differently, and the moment you re-establish Canadian tax residency, Canada's rules take priority.

WHAT CHANGES WHEN YOU MOVE BACK TO CANADA

Once you are a Canadian tax resident again, Canada taxes you on your worldwide income. That includes withdrawals from

U.S. retirement plans—even if those plans were accumulated entirely while you lived in the United States.

The Canada–U.S. tax treaty helps reduce double taxation, but it does not eliminate tax altogether, and it does not preserve U.S.-style tax treatment.

IRA AND 401(K) WITHDRAWALS

When you live in Canada:

- Withdrawals from IRAs and 401(k)s are generally taxable in Canada as ordinary income.

- For a non-U.S. person receiving periodic IRA or 401(k) distributions, the U.S. generally withholds 15% under the Canada–U.S. tax treaty.
- A lump-sum IRA distribution to a non-U.S. person may be subject to 30% U.S. withholding.
- If withdrawals are taken before age 59½, an additional 10% early-withdrawal penalty may also apply.
- If you are still a U.S. citizen or green card holder, the U.S. tax treatment is different: the distribution may be taxable on your U.S. return, not merely subject to treaty withholding.
- You report the full withdrawal on your Canadian tax return.
- U.S. tax paid or withheld may generally be claimed as a foreign tax credit in Canada, but the credit must be calculated and reported correctly.

The key point is that Canada taxes the gross withdrawal once you are a Canadian tax resident. A non-U.S. person is generally dealing with U.S. withholding on the distribution, while a U.S. citizen or green card holder may also have ongoing U.S. tax filing obligations on the gross amount.

Timing withdrawals carefully becomes essential.

ROTH IRAS — THE MOST COMMON TRAP

Roth IRAs are widely misunderstood by returning Canadians.

In the U.S., qualified Roth withdrawals are tax-free. In Canada, that tax-free status does not automatically carry over.

To preserve Roth tax-free treatment in Canada, specific elections and disclosures must be made—generally in the first year you become a Canadian resident again. If those steps are missed, Canada may treat the Roth as a taxable investment account.

A REAL STORY: THE ROTH IRA SURPRISE

A Calgary couple returned after twenty years in Texas. They had been told their Roth IRA was "tax-free for life."

In Canada, it wasn't.

Because they failed to complete the required filings in their first year back, Canada could treat future Roth growth and withdrawals as taxable unless the treaty election issue was corrected. In some cases, CRA may allow a late-filed Roth election, but that relief can be compromised if contributions are made to the Roth after becoming a Canadian resident.

The mistake was not aggressive planning—it was assuming the Roth's U.S. status automatically applied in Canada.

U.S. SOCIAL SECURITY BENEFITS

Social Security is treated more favourably under the tax treaty:

- Canada taxes only 85% of U.S. Social Security benefits
- The United States generally does not tax Social Security once you reside in Canada
- Benefits are reported on your Canadian return, not a
- U.S. return

This often surprises returnees who expect U.S. withholding to continue.

WHY ADVANCE PLANNING MATTERS

The year you return to Canada is the most important year for retirement planning decisions. Actions taken—or missed—during that year can permanently change how your U.S. retirement assets are taxed.

Key decisions include:

- Whether to withdraw funds before returning
- How to structure Roth elections
- How to coordinate foreign tax credits
- How withdrawals interact with Canadian marginal tax rates

These decisions are difficult to unwind later.

KEY TAKEAWAY

U.S. retirement accounts do not "carry their tax rules with them" when you move back to Canada. Canada will tax them according to Canadian law, with limited treaty relief.

Understanding this shift—and planning for it before or during the return year—can prevent permanent and expensive mistakes.

HEALTHCARE SHOCK — WHAT HAPPENS TO U.S. MEDICAL INSURANCE WHEN YOU LEAVE

Healthcare is one of the most underestimated risks when Canadians return home from the United States. Many assume coverage simply switches back on once they cross the border. In reality, the move often creates a coverage gap at the moment continuity matters most.

This section explains what happens to U.S. medical insurance when you leave, how Canadian coverage restarts, and why the transition has to be planned rather than assumed.

MEDICARE: IT DOES NOT TRAVEL WITH YOU

Medicare is designed for U.S. residents. Once you no longer live in the United States, it generally stops serving as meaningful protection.

Key realities returnees often miss:

- U.S. Medicare generally cannot be used in Canada
- Routine care outside the U.S. is not covered
- Many Medicare Advantage and Part D plans terminate when residency changes
- Dropping Medicare can create late re-enrollment
- penalties if you later return to the U.S. system

Some returning Canadians keep paying Medicare premiums for years just in case, not realizing the coverage provides little or no benefit outside the United States.

What remains often becomes a sunk cost rather than a safety net.

PRIVATE U.S. HEALTH INSURANCE: OFTEN INVALID AFTER DEPARTURE

Private U.S. health insurance is usually tied to U.S. residency.

Once you move back to Canada:

- Coverage may terminate automatically
- Claims incurred outside the U.S. are often denied
- Networks, providers, and emergency coverage may no longer apply

Many policies stop working the moment residency changes, even if premiums continue to be paid.

That creates a dangerous assumption gap.

CANADIAN HEALTHCARE: THE WAITING PERIOD REALITY

Canadian provincial healthcare does not always restart immediately.

Most provinces impose a waiting period—often up to three months—before full coverage resumes. During that time, returning Canadians are expected to carry private insurance.

Common requirements include:

- Proof of residency re-establishment
- Application and reinstatement processing
- Documentation of prior coverage and status

The waiting period varies by province, but the risk remains the same.

A REAL STORY: THE THREE-MONTH GAP

A woman returning to Ontario assumed OHIP coverage would restart immediately.

One week after arrival, she fainted and was hospitalized. She later learned her provincial coverage had not yet resumed. The hospital bill was entirely out of pocket.

The shock was not the illness. It was discovering there was no safety net.

THE OVERLOOKED TRANSITION WINDOW

The most exposed period is the gap between systems:

- U.S. coverage winding down or no longer valid
- Canadian coverage not yet active

Without planning, returnees can find themselves uninsured on both sides of the border at the same time.

This is especially risky for older Canadians and those with ongoing medical needs.

PRACTICAL PLANNING CONSIDERATIONS

Before returning to Canada, individuals should:

- Confirm exactly when U.S. coverage ends
- Understand provincial waiting periods
- Arrange temporary private coverage for the transition
- Transfer medical records and prescriptions
- Identify Canadian healthcare providers in advance

Healthcare transitions require coordination, not assumptions.

KEY TAKEAWAY

Returning to Canada does not mean healthcare protection automatically resumes. U.S. coverage often stops quietly, while Canadian coverage may take months to activate.

The safest return is a planned one—where healthcare continuity is addressed before the move, not after an emergency.

YOUR FIRST-YEAR CANADIAN FILING — THE T1135 TRAP

For many returning Canadians, the first Canadian tax return after moving home is the most complex filing they will ever complete. It is also the return where mistakes are least forgiven.

The issue is not tax owing. The issue is disclosure.

Canada's foreign reporting rules apply immediately once you re-establish Canadian tax residency, even if your return year feels transitional or incomplete.

WHY THE FIRST RETURN IS DIFFERENT

Once CRA considers you a Canadian resident again, you must report:

- Worldwide income
- Worldwide assets
- Foreign financial relationships

This obligation begins on your residency reactivation date, not at year-end and not when life "settles down."

Many returnees underestimate how quickly these obligations resume.

THE T1135: FOREIGN INCOME VERIFICATION STATEMENT

One of the most overlooked requirements is Form T1135, which applies if you own specified foreign property with a total cost exceeding $100,000 CAD at any point during the year.

Specified foreign property includes:

- U.S. bank accounts
- U.S. brokerage accounts
- U.S. rental properties
- Interests in partnerships or LLCs
- Certain U.S. trusts
- Foreign investment accounts

It does not matter whether the assets earned income. Ownership alone can trigger the filing.

WHY THIS TRAP IS SO COMMON

Returning Canadians often assume that accounts already known to U.S. institutions or tax authorities do not need separate disclosure in Canada.

They do.

CRA's concern is not whether the assets were taxed properly elsewhere. It is whether they are disclosed properly for the tax year in which Canadian residency resumes, usually through Form T1135 filed with the Canadian tax return the following year. For most individuals, that deadline is generally April 30.

A REAL STORY: THE "FORGOTTEN BANK ACCOUNT" PENALTY

A Toronto resident returned from Arizona and failed to disclose a U.S. bank account holding approximately $120,000 USD.

- The account was inactive.
- The income was minimal.

U.S. taxes had been paid properly.

CRA assessed a $2,500 penalty for failure to file Form T1135. The penalty was not based on intent. It was automatic.

COMMON FILING ERRORS IN THE RETURN YEAR

Returning Canadians frequently make the following mistakes:

- Forgetting to disclose U.S. accounts that remain open
- Assuming joint accounts or spousal accounts are exempt
- Misunderstanding cost base versus market value
- Filing T1135 late or not at all
- Assuming their accountant "will handle it" without flagging assets

In CRA's system, omission equals non-compliance, regardless of intent.

WHY PENALTIES ARE SO SEVERE

CRA treats foreign asset disclosure as a compliance priority.

Penalties can apply even where no additional tax is owing. Once a filing is missed, the issue quickly becomes one of non-compliance rather than tax calculation.

PRACTICAL STEPS FOR A CLEAN FIRST-YEAR FILING

Before filing your first Canadian return after returning:

- Inventory every U.S. account and asset
- Identify cost bases in Canadian dollars
- Determine which assets trigger T1135 reporting

- Coordinate U.S. and Canadian filings for consistency
- Work with a cross-border tax professional familiar with return years

Preparation matters more in this year than any other.

KEY TAKEAWAY

The first Canadian tax return after returning home is not routine. It is a disclosure-heavy transition filing where even small oversights can lead to disproportionate penalties.

Accuracy, completeness, and coordination are essential.

RRSP REINSTATEMENT — WHAT YOU CAN AND CANNOT DO

Returning to Canada reactivates your ability to take advantage of registered retirement accounts, but it does not reset or restore contribution room or the years you were non-resident. This distinction is one of the most misunderstood aspects of returning home.

Many Canadians assume that time spent earning income in the United States somehow translates into RRSP room once they are back. It does not.

WHAT HAPPENS TO YOUR RRSP WHILE YOU LIVE IN THE U.S.

While you are a non-resident of Canada:

- Your RRSP contribution room generally does not grow from U.S. employment income earned while you are non-resident.You generally cannot make new contributions in excess of your RRSP limit. Existing RRSPs may remain invested but inactive
- Income can continue to grow tax-free at the U.S. federal level under the Canada–U.S. tax treaty.
- Some U.S. states, such as California, do not recognize the same treaty-based deferral and will tax RRSP income or growth under state rules.

The RRSP system is tied to Canadian employment income and Canadian residency. Time outside the country pauses contribution room.

WHAT CHANGES WHEN YOU RETURN

Once Canadian tax residency is re-established:

- You regain the ability to contribute to an RRSP
- New contribution room is created only by Canadian employment income
- New RRSP contribution room is created according to CRA's formula, which is based on prior-year Canadian-source employment income, so the amount of room available for the current year may depend on income earned in Canada after your return. You may not be able to contribute the full amount until the following year if prior-year income was limited.
- Past unused room carries forward, but no new room is added retroactively

U.S. income earned while non-resident does not create RRSP room.

A REAL STORY: THE OVERCONTRIBUTION

A woman returning from Seattle assumed that her U.S. salary over several years generated RRSP room.

It did not.

She contributed $14,000 based on an incorrect assumption and later received a CRA notice assessing excess contribution penalties. She was forced to request discretionary relief and unwind part of the contribution.

The mistake was not aggressive—it was common.

WHY OVERCONTRIBUTIONS ARE SO EASY TO MAKE

The confusion usually arises because:

- RRSP room feels automatic to long-time Canadians
- Notices of Assessment may not reflect return-year changes immediately
- Financial institutions do not verify eligibility before accepting contributions

- U.S. income feels "earned," even though it does not qualify

CRA does not consider intent when applying excess contribution penalties.

WITHDRAWALS AFTER RETURNING

Once you are resident again:

- RRSP withdrawals are fully taxable in Canada
- Withholding applies at source
- Withdrawals do not create new contribution room

Timing withdrawals incorrectly can push income into higher tax brackets or disrupt benefit eligibility.

PLANNING CONSIDERATIONS FOR RETURNING CANADIANS

Before contributing or withdrawing after returning:

- Confirm your updated RRSP room with CRA
- Distinguish between unused room and newly generated room
- Coordinate RRSP decisions with U.S. account withdrawals
- Avoid contributions until residency status is clearly established

When in doubt, delay contributions rather than assume eligibility.

KEY TAKEAWAY

Returning to Canada allows you to resume your RRSP—but only under Canadian rules. The RRSP account itself remains open while you are a non-resident. U.S. income does not count, and past years spent as a non-resident do not generate new contribution room. Overcontributions are penalized quickly.Careful verification protects you from an avoidable and frustrating mistake.

U.S. RENTAL PROPERTY — THE OBLIGATION THAT DOESN'T END

Returning to Canada does not end your relationship with U.S. tax authorities if you are a non-U.S. resident and continue to own U.S. rental property. Many Canadians assume that once they move home, their U.S.

obligations naturally wind down. Rental real estate is one of the clearest examples of why that assumption fails.

Ownership alone keeps you in the U.S. system.

WHY U.S. RENTAL P.ROPERTY IS DIFFERENT

U.S. rental property creates an ongoing nexus with the United States, regardless of where you live. Once you return to Canada, the property does not become passive in a regulatory sense. It remains subject to U.S. federal and state tax rules until it is sold.

As a non-resident owner, you are generally required to continue:

- Filing U.S. federal non-resident returns (Form 1040NR)
- Filing applicable state tax returns
- Reporting rental income and expenses
- Tracking annual depreciation
- Maintaining records in U.S. dollars

These obligations resume automatically each year.

DEPRECIATION: THE SILENT ACCUMULATOR

One of the most misunderstood aspects of U.S. rental ownership is depreciation.

Even if depreciation reduces or eliminates annual taxable income, it is not optional. The IRS expects it to be claimed, and whether or not you do, it accumulates in the background.

That accumulation matters later.

A REAL STORY: DEPRECIATION RECAPTURE SHOCK

A Montreal resident sold his Scottsdale rental property several years after returning to Canada. He had owned the property for over a decade and had claimed depreciation annually while filing

U.S. returns.

At sale, he learned that:

- Every dollar of depreciation claimed over twelve years
- Was subject to U.S. depreciation recapture tax
- At a federal rate of up to 25 percent

The recapture alone eliminated nearly half of the perceived profit on the sale.

The shock was not the tax—it was learning too late that it was inevitable.

FOREIGN INVESTMENT IN REAL PROPERTY TAX ACT (FIRPTA): WITHHOLDING AT THE TIME OF SALE

When a non-resident sells U.S. real estate, FIRPTA rules apply. Under FIRPTA:

- A portion of the gross sale price is withheld at closing
- Withholding is not based on profit
- Refunds require post-sale filings
- Timing mismatches can create cash-flow strain

Many sellers are surprised to see tens or hundreds of thousands withheld even when the transaction is economically modest.

CANADIAN TAX IMPLICATIONS DO NOT REPLACE U.S. ONES

Selling or holding U.S. rental property also triggers Canadian considerations:

- Capital gains reporting in Canada
- Foreign tax credit coordination
- Currency conversion effects on gains
- Timing mismatches between U.S. and Canadian filings

Returning home does not consolidate these systems. It doubles the coordination requirement.

WHY THIS OBLIGATION IS OFTEN OVERLOOKED

Returning Canadians frequently underestimate rental obligations because:

- The property feels "managed" by a third party
- Income may be minimal or break-even
- They assume the obligation ended with residency change

- Their focus shifts to settling back into Canada

None of these reduce U.S. filing requirements.

PLANNING CONSIDERATIONS FOR RETURNEES WITH U.S. PROPERTY

Before returning—or soon after—you should:

- Confirm ongoing U.S. filing obligations
- Evaluate whether continued ownership makes sense
- Model depreciation recapture before selling
- Plan FIRPTA withholding and liquidity needs
- Coordinate Canadian and U.S. tax timelines

Ignoring the issue does not make it disappear. It compounds it.

KEY TAKEAWAY

U.S. rental property creates obligations that follow you home. Depreciation, filings, and withholding rules continue long after you cross the border.

For returning Canadians, rental real estate requires deliberate planning—not passive neglect.

POST-DEPARTURE U.S. FILINGS — YOU STILL HAVE OBLIGATIONS

One of the most persistent misunderstandings among returning Canadians is the belief that leaving the United States ends all U.S. tax and reporting responsibilities. In reality, certain filings may still be required even after you are no longer a U.S. citizen, green card holder, or resident. For those who retain U.S. person status, full U.S. tax returns must continue to be filed. Understanding your specific status and obligations is essential to avoid unexpected penalties or compliance issues.

Leaving the country changes how you file, not always *whether* you file.

WHY OBLIGATIONS CONTINUE AFTER YOU LEAVE

U.S. tax and reporting requirements are tied to income, assets, and prior activity, not physical presence alone. Even after re-establishing Canadian residency, you may still have U.S. filing responsibilities if income, assets, or reporting connections remain in place.

These obligations can continue for years.

COMMON POST-DEPARTURE FILINGS

Returning Canadians are often required to continue filing:

- U.S. non-resident tax returns (Form 1040NR) for U.S.-source income
- State tax returns, particularly where property or income remains
- FIRPTA filings when selling U.S. real estate
- Dual-status returns in the year of departure
- Partnership or LLC filings, if ownership continues

Each filing has its own deadline, penalty structure, and documentation requirements.

A FINAL STORY: THE ARIZONA PENSION WORKER

A Canadian who worked in Arizona for eighteen years returned home believing his U.S. tax obligations had ended. He was not a U.S. citizen and had never held a green card, but because he had earned U.S.-source income and remained connected to the U.S. tax system, certain filings were still required. The distinction between former U.S. persons and those who retain U.S. person status directly determined the scope of his filing responsibilities.

It was not.

Because he continued receiving pension income and still owned

U.S. rental property, he was required to file U.S. federal and state returns for two additional years. Failure to do so would have triggered penalties and interest.

The problem was not complexity. It was assumption.

WHY THESE FILINGS ARE OFTEN MISSED

Post-departure obligations are commonly overlooked because:

- Income arrives automatically
- Assets remain unchanged year to year
- Mail and notices stop reaching U.S. addresses
- Focus shifts entirely to Canadian filings

Unfortunately, the IRS and state authorities do not treat silence as closure.

PLANNING CONSIDERATIONS FOR A CLEAN EXIT

Before and after returning to Canada:

- Identify all continuing U.S.-source income
- Determine which filings remain required
- Coordinate departure-year returns carefully
- Align U.S. and Canadian reporting for consistency
- Close or restructure U.S. entities where appropriate

A clean return depends on controlled disengagement, not assumption.

KEY TAKEAWAY

Some U.S. filing obligations can continue after you return to Canada, especially where income, property, or reporting connections remain in place.

Identifying those obligations early is what prevents avoidable problems later.

CONCLUSION — PLANNING IS THE ONLY WAY TO RETURN SMOOTHLY

Returning to Canada is not simply an emotional or logistical transition. It is a technical one that unfolds across two tax systems, two healthcare frameworks, and multiple regulatory timelines.

The traps outlined in this chapter are not the result of aggressive planning or risky behaviour. They arise from reasonable assumptions made in the absence of clear guidance.

Nearly all of them are avoidable.

By understanding how departure and return are treated by both countries, coordinating filings properly, and planning transitions in advance, returning Canadians can move home with confidence rather than correction.

A return home should feel like a closing chapter. With proper planning, it can be.

CHAPTER 3
TRANSPORTING WEALTH ACROSS THE BORDER: WHY YOUR MONEY NEEDS ITS OWN IMMIGRATION PLAN

In This Chapter, You Will Learn...

In this chapter, you will learn why moving money across the Canada–U.S. border requires the same level of planning and precision as moving your life.

Specifically, this chapter explains:

- Why U.S. retirement accounts do not automatically adapt when Canadian residency resumes
- How IRAs, 401(k)s, Roth IRAs, pensions, RRSPs, RSUs, and savings are taxed once you move back to Canada
- What happens when U.S. brokerages restrict or freeze accounts after a change of address
- Why Roth IRAs can lose their tax-free status without a timely treaty election
- How RRSPs are treated for U.S. residents and what changes upon returning to Canada
- Where double taxation commonly arises with deferred compensation and equity plans
- How PFIC rules turn ordinary Canadian investments into major tax liabilities for U.S. persons
- Why currency conversion costs silently erode retirement savings
- How Required Minimum Distributions continue regardless of where you live
- The real-world mistakes returning Canadians make when financial migration is not planned
- Practical steps to move retirement assets and savings across borders with clarity and control

This chapter sets out the financial realities that follow you home—and shows why your wealth needs its own immigration plan.

WHY MOVING YOUR MONEY IS HARDER THAN MOVING YOURSELF

Many Canadians assume that once they have successfully crossed the border back into Canada, the hardest part of the move is behind them. The boxes are unpacked. The vehicles are registered. The address is changed. Life resumes.

But for those returning with U.S. retirement accounts, brokerage assets, pensions, and long-built savings, the more complicated part often begins after arrival.

Unlike immigration, which has a clear moment of entry, money does not cross borders cleanly. Financial systems operate on residency status, reporting obligations, treaty elections, custodial rules, and tax classifications that do not reset simply because you moved. Each account carries its own history, its own governing rules, and its own exposure when residency changes.

People often spend months organizing movers, property sales, and the physical return home, while assuming their savings will adjust on their own. They do not.

The result is often costly:

- Accounts become restricted or frozen
- Tax-deferred plans lose their intended treatment
- Income is taxed twice under mismatched systems
- Currency conversion quietly erodes capital
- Reporting obligations surface years later

What makes these outcomes especially frustrating is that they are rarely caused by reckless decisions. More often, they result from missing information, misunderstood treaty rules, and timing errors that are difficult to correct later.

WHY THIS CHAPTER MATTERS

When you return to Canada, you are not simply changing where you live. You are also changing how retirement vehicles, investment accounts, and deferred benefits are classified, taxed, and reported.

This applies to:

- IRAs and 401(k)s built over decades
- Roth IRAs that appear tax-free but are not automatically protected
- RRSPs that behaved one way while you were a U.S. resident and another when you return
- Pensions, RSUs, and deferred compensation that straddle two tax systems
- U.S. brokerage accounts subject to residency-based restrictions
- Savings held in U.S. dollars that must eventually be converted

Each of these assets reacts differently to a change in residency. Treating them as a single pool of "retirement money" is one of the most common and expensive mistakes returning Canadians make.

THE REAL STORIES OF CROSS-BORDER FINANCIAL MISTAKES

The risks of moving money across the border are easiest to understand when seen through real outcomes rather than theory. The following stories are not outliers. They represent patterns that appear repeatedly when people return to Canada without a coordinated financial migration plan.

Each case illustrates a different failure point, but they all share a common thread: the assumption that existing accounts would continue to behave the same way after residency changed.

They did not.

STORY 1 — THE ROTH IRA THAT LOST ITS MAGIC

Emily returned to Canada with what she believed was her most secure asset: a Roth IRA worth approximately $300,000. She had spent years contributing under U.S. rules, carefully building what she understood to be tax-free retirement income.

What she did not know was that the Roth's treatment would depend not just on the account itself, but on what was done after her return to Canada.

Her accountant did not file the required treaty election. The consequences were permanent:

- CRA treated the Roth as a taxable account
- All future growth became taxable in Canada
- Withdrawals lost their tax-free status
- The election could not be filed retroactively because she continued to make Roth contributions after her arrival to Canada.

Emily summed it up simply:

"I thought the whole point of a Roth was that it was protected."

She lost more than $70,000 in long-term tax advantages, not because of investment performance, but because a cross-border protection step was missed when her residency changed.

STORY 2 — THE ENGINEER WHO PAID TWICE

Tom worked in the United States for several years but kept his RRSP intact in Canada. While living in the U.S., he withdrew $20,000 from the account, assuming the process would be straightforward.

Instead, the withdrawal triggered consequences on both sides of the border:

- Canada applied 25% non-resident withholding tax
- The IRS treated the withdrawal as taxable income
- Required U.S. foreign tax credit reporting forms were missed
- Penalties followed

Tom later said:

"Withdrawing money was harder than filing my tax return."

The problem was not the RRSP alone. It was what happened when a Canadian account and U.S. tax residency collided without coordination.

STORY 3 — RSUS TAXED IN TWO COUNTRIES

Adam relocated from San Francisco to Vancouver while holding restricted stock units from his employer. The RSUs continued vesting after his return.

Neither his U.S. nor Canadian advisor coordinated the treaty treatment.

The result:

- Canada taxed the income as employment compensation
- The U.S. also taxed the same income as U.S.-sourced
- No proper credits were claimed
- Adam overpaid by $48,000

Deferred compensation is one of the most complex areas of cross-border planning. When vesting schedules, residency changes, and treaty rules intersect, small mistakes become expensive very quickly.

STORY 4 — THE FROZEN BROKERAGE ACCOUNT

Helen, a U.S. citizen, did what she believed was responsible. She updated her U.S. brokerage account with her new Canadian address. Because she remained a U.S. person, her account remained subject to U.S. regulatory oversight and reporting requirements, and certain actions—including liquidations—could still trigger U.S. tax consequences despite her re-established Canadian residency.

Within forty-eight hours, the account was restricted. She could sell, but not buy. And she was forced to close the account.

The forced liquidation created a chain reaction:

- Capital gains were triggered
- Taxable income spiked
- OAS clawback followed
- Long-term investment strategy was disrupted

Helen described it perfectly:

"This wasn't a market loss. It was a paperwork loss."

U.S. brokerage firms often restrict accounts once clients become non-residents. This is not a tax issue alone. It is a custodial and regulatory one, and it frequently catches returnees off guard.

STORY 5 — THE PFIC NIGHTMARE

Jason, a U.S. citizen living in Toronto, invested in simple Canadian mutual funds.

Under U.S. tax law, those funds were classified as Passive Foreign Investment Companies (PFICs), triggering one of the most punitive reporting regimes in the tax code.

The outcome:

- A U.S. tax return exceeding 200 pages
- Thousands in additional tax
- A $3,000 annual preparation bill

PFIC rules exist regardless of intent or investment size. Many people discover them only after filing becomes unavoidable.

WHY THESE STORIES MATTER

These stories involve different accounts, different rules, and different mistakes. What connects them is timing.

Once residency changes, missed elections, delayed filings, and account restrictions become much harder to fix.

THE CURRENCY CONVERSION TRAP

One of the most underestimated risks in a cross-border move is currency conversion. Unlike taxes or frozen accounts, currency losses rarely arrive as notices or penalties. They happen quietly, instantly, and without appeal.

Many returning Canadians assume currency conversion is a mechanical step—something that simply needs to be done. In reality, how and when money is converted often determines whether thousands of dollars are preserved or lost.

HOW CURRENCY LOSSES REALLY OCCUR

Most people focus on exchange rates without realizing that the real cost lies in spreads, not headlines.

When large sums are converted through major banks:

- The posted rate is not the rate you receive
- A hidden spread of 2%–3% is common
- The loss is embedded in the transaction, not itemized

Because the cost is invisible, it often goes unnoticed.

A REAL EXAMPLE: THE $9,000 THAT VANISHED INSTANTLY

Mark and Linda converted $300,000 USD through a Canadian bank shortly after returning home.

They assumed:

- Their long-standing bank relationship meant fair pricing
- The difference between institutions would be marginal

What actually happened:

- A 3% spread was applied
- $9,000 disappeared immediately
- No receipt explained the loss

Another couple converting proceeds from a U.S. home sale lost over $21,000 the same way.

These were not speculative investments gone wrong. They were routine conversions handled without strategy.

WHY TIMING MATTERS MORE THAN PEOPLE EXPECT

Currency conversion mistakes are often compounded by urgency.

Returning Canadians frequently convert funds:

- Immediately after moving
- During emotionally stressful periods
- Without evaluating alternatives

- Without separating short-term needs from long-term assets

This leads to large, one-time conversions at unfavourable rates instead of staged or strategic transfers.

BETTER CURRENCY PRACTICES ALREADY EXIST

Specialized foreign exchange providers and structured transfer strategies typically charge:

- Between 0.20% and 1.0%
- With transparent pricing
- With settlement timing flexibility

On large balances, the difference between a bank spread and a structured FX approach often exceeds the cost of professional planning itself.

WHY CURRENCY ERRORS ARE PERMANENT

Unlike tax filings, currency mistakes cannot be amended.

Once converted:

- The loss is realized
- There is no credit, deduction, or recovery
- Future planning cannot undo the damage

This is why currency management must be treated as a planning decision, not an administrative task.

THE DEEPER ISSUE

Currency losses often occur because money moves faster than advice.

People plan immigration.

They plan housing.

They plan logistics.

But currency is moved reactively, at the last moment, when decisions are rushed.

In cross-border planning, silence around currency is often the most expensive oversight.

REQUIRED MINIMUM DISTRIBUTIONS — THE TAX OBLIGATION THAT FOLLOWS YOU HOME

Many returning Canadians assume that once they leave the United States, U.S. retirement rules stop applying. Required Minimum Distributions (RMDs) prove otherwise.

RMDs do not follow residency. They follow the account. WHAT RMDS ACTUALLY ARE

RMDs are mandatory withdrawals from certain U.S. retirement accounts once you reach the required age (currently tied to U.S. federal law thresholds).

They apply to:

- Traditional IRAs
- 401(k)s and similar employer plans

They do not apply to Roth IRAs during the original owner's lifetime

Once you reach the age in which you must start taking RMDs:

- Must be taken annually
- Cannot be deferred
- Cannot be rolled into an RRSP
- Cannot be ignored because you live in Canada

A REAL STORY: THE LETTER THAT ARRIVED TOO LATE

Don returned to Vancouver Island at age 73, confident that his

U.S. obligations were behind him.

Then the IRS letter arrived:

"Your Required Minimum Distribution is due."

Don was surprised for two reasons:

1. He believed RMDs only applied while living in the U.S.
2. He assumed Canadian residency changed the rules

Neither assumption was correct.

HOW RMDS ARE TAXED AFTER YOU RETURN TO CANADA

When you are a Canadian resident:

- The U.S. withholds tax on the RMD (generally 15% under the treaty) as a non-resident of the U.S. and non-U.S. person
- Canada taxes the full withdrawal as income
- A foreign tax credit is allowed under the treaty and can be claimed on your Canadian tax return to avoid double taxation; however, errors in correctly claiming the credit are common

The result is often:

- Higher marginal tax rates
- Increased taxable income in Canada
- Exposure to OAS clawback

RMDs frequently push retirees into income levels they never planned for.

WHY RMDS CATCH PEOPLE OFF GUARD

RMDs are particularly disruptive because:

- They are mandatory, not elective
- They arrive later in life, when planning flexibility is lower
- They are easy to forget during the chaos of a move
- They often coincide with other income sources (CPP, OAS, RRIFs)

By the time the issue surfaces, the options are limited.

THE PLANNING GAP

Many people plan:

- When to return
- Where to live
- How to move assets

But they do not plan:

- How RMDs will interact with Canadian tax brackets
- How withdrawals will affect government benefits
- Whether earlier restructuring could have reduced exposure

This gap is costly—not because the rules are unfair, but because they are often misunderstood.

THE CORE LESSON

RMDs, Roth IRAs, and cross-border investments are **known obligations.** The real mistake is treating them as though Canadian residency automatically changes U.S. rules:

- **RMDs** must still be reported to the U.S., even after returning to Canada, if the individual is a U.S. person. Non-U.S. persons may have withholding obligations.
- **Roth IRAs** may require treaty elections to preserve tax treatment; failure to act can trigger Canadian taxation of future growth, though relief may still be possible if no post-arrival contributions were made.
- **U.S. mutual funds and retirement accounts** may not be held in Canadian accounts due to regulatory restrictions; proper placement and planning prevent forced liquidation or account freezes.
- **Currency and cross-border cash flow planning** is essential to prevent unnecessary losses from timing mismatches or exchange rate spreads.

The key takeaway: **coordination across U.S. and Canadian systems is critical**. Proper planning avoids predictable mistakes, stabilizes portfolios, and protects assets while ensuring compliance in both countries.

U.S. RENTAL PROPERTY — THE OBLIGATION THAT DOESN'T END AT THE BORDER

For many returning Canadians, selling a U.S. home feels like the final step in closing a chapter of life abroad. When that property has ever been rented, however, the tax relationship with the United States often continues long after the move is complete.

U.S. rental property does not reset when you change residency. It follows you home.

WHY RENTAL PROPERTY CREATES ONGOING U.S. OBLIGATIONS

Owning U.S. rental real estate ties you to the U.S. tax system regardless of where you live. Even after returning to Canada, you remain subject to U.S. reporting and tax rules connected to that property.

Common ongoing obligations include:

- Filing U.S. non-resident tax returns (Form 1040-NR)
- Filing state tax returns where the property is located
- Reporting rental income and expenses annually
- Tracking accumulated depreciation
- Complying with FIRPTA rules upon sale

Many Canadians mistakenly believe that once they are no longer U.S. residents, these requirements disappear. They do not.

WHY DEPRECIATION IS SO DANGEROUS

Depreciation feels invisible while you own the property. It quietly reduces taxable rental income year after year. But it never disappears.

When the property is sold:

- All accumulated depreciation becomes taxable
- The tax is triggered even if the property lost value
- The obligation exists even if you live in Canada

Depreciation is not optional retroactively. Once claimed—or deemed claimed—it must be accounted for.

CANADIAN TAX ADDS ANOTHER LAYER

When a Canadian resident sells U.S. rental property:

- Canada also taxes the capital gain
- A foreign tax credit is available for U.S. tax paid, which generally eliminates timing mismatches for personally held property, since foreign income is reported and the credit is claimed in the same tax year

- Timing mismatches may occur only if the property is held in a U.S. revocable living trust or LLC, in which case the foreign tax credit may not perfectly align with Canadian reporting
- The result can be:
- Double taxation on part of the gain
- Higher effective tax rates than expected
- Reduced net proceeds after sale

Without coordination, even well-intentioned reporting can lead to avoidable losses.

THE CORE LESSON

U.S. rental property creates a long tail of responsibility.

Moving back to Canada does not end:

- U.S. filing requirements
- Depreciation consequences
- State-level obligations
- Reporting complexity

The mistake is not owning the property.

The mistake is assuming the rules stop when residency changes.

WHEN BROKERAGE ACCOUNTS FREEZE — THE COMPLIANCE SHOCK NO ONE WARNS YOU ABOUT

For many returning Canadians, the first real sign that money does not move as freely as people do comes without a letter, a phone call, or an explanation.

It comes as a login error.

Or a notice that says, *"Your account has been restricted."*

WHY U.S. BROKERAGES FREEZE ACCOUNTS WHEN YOU MOVE TO CANADA

U.S. financial institutions are governed by strict securities, licensing, and residency rules. When your legal address changes from the United States to Canada, many brokerages are no longer authorized to service you in the same way.

From their perspective, this is not a relationship issue—it is a compliance issue.

Once your address changes:

- The brokerage may no longer be licensed to provide services to a Canadian resident
- Investment advice rules change
- Product availability changes
- Reporting obligations change

The default response is often restriction.

WHAT "RESTRICTED" USUALLY MEANS IN PRACTICE

A restricted account is not always closed—but it is rarely usable in the way it was before.

Common restrictions include:

- You may be allowed to sell, but not buy
- Automatic reinvestment may stop
- New contributions may be blocked
- Certain holdings may be forced to liquidate

Account features may be disabled without notice This often occurs within days of updating your address.

WHY DOING "NOTHING" CAN BE WORSE THAN DOING IT WRONG

Some people delay changing their address to avoid restrictions. That approach carries its own risks:

- Incorrect tax reporting
- Inconsistent residency records
- Compliance issues if discovered later
- Problems during audits or estate administration

The real problem is not disclosure.

It is disclosure without a plan.

THE STRUCTURAL PROBLEM BEHIND THE FREEZE

Brokerage freezes are not personal. They are structural.

Most U.S. platforms:

- Are built for U.S. residents
- Are not licensed to advise or transact for Canadians
- Default to restriction rather than risk

This is why returning Canadians often feel punished for doing the right thing.

THE PLANNING LESSON

Your investment accounts need their own relocation strategy.

Before updating addresses or triggering compliance reviews, returning Canadians should understand:

- Which accounts will be restricted
- Which assets may need to move
- Which structures remain valid in Canada
- What timing minimizes disruption

Once an account is frozen, your options shrink dramatically.

YOUR MONEY NEEDS ITS OWN IMMIGRATION PLAN

The stories in this chapter point to one clear conclusion: crossing the border without a financial migration plan creates avoidable damage.

People plan the move itself. What they often do not plan is how assets built under one system behave once residency changes.

WHAT GOES WRONG WITHOUT PLANNING

When money crosses the border without structure, predictable problems appear:

- Roth IRAs lose their tax-free status
- IRAs and 401(k)s are taxed twice or withheld incorrectly
- RRSPs trigger unexpected reporting or penalties
- Brokerage accounts freeze after address changes
- RSUs and deferred compensation are taxed by both countries
- Pension rollovers are missed entirely
- PFIC rules turn ordinary investments into tax disasters
- Currency conversion quietly erodes years of savings
- Required Minimum Distributions arrive on schedule, regardless of residency

None of these outcomes are rare. They are routine.

What makes them costly is not complexity—it is timing. Most of these mistakes cannot be undone after the first filing year.

WHY FINANCIAL IMMIGRATION IS HARDER THAN PHYSICAL IMMIGRATION

People move on dates. Financial systems react to triggers.

Residency changes, elections, reporting rules, and account restrictions do not all move at the same pace. That is why people often feel they made the move successfully, only to discover later that their assets did not.

THE CENTRAL LESSON OF THIS CHAPTER

Wealth does not migrate automatically. It has to be guided.

A clean financial return depends on understanding how accounts will be treated after residency changes, what elections must be made on time, and which obligations continue after the move.

A BETTER WAY FORWARD

These stories are not meant to create fear. They show what happens when planning is delayed.

With preparation, many of these problems can be avoided, and returning home can feel like relief rather than repair.

CHAPTER 4
AMERICANS MOVING TO CANADA: A TAX, IMMIGRATION, AND FINANCIAL RESET

In This Chapter, You Will Learn...

In this chapter, you will learn why moving from the United States to Canada is not a simple relocation, but a full financial and regulatory reset that affects nearly every aspect of financial life.

Specifically, this chapter explains:

- How Americans often become Canadian tax residents without realizing it
- Why U.S. citizens remain subject to IRS taxation and reporting for life, regardless of where they live
- How Canadian investments trigger PFIC rules for Americans and why those penalties are so severe
- Where RSUs, stock options, and deferred compensation commonly create double taxation
- Why U.S. life insurance policies frequently break under Canadian tax law
- The cost-of-living differences Americans rarely anticipate before moving north
- When foreign asset reporting (FBAR, FATCA, Form 8938) begins and why it is unavoidable
- Why U.S. brokerage accounts often freeze or restrict activity after a Canadian address update
- How small, uncoordinated mistakes compound into major financial disruption
- Why integrated cross-border planning is essential to rebuilding a stable financial structure in Canada

This chapter shows why Americans moving to Canada need more than good intentions — they need a coordinated strategy that accounts for two tax systems, two regulatory regimes, and one integrated life.

THE DAY DAVID BECAME A CANADIAN TAX RESIDENT (WITHOUT REALIZING IT)

David arrived in Toronto from Seattle on a TN visa, planning to "see how it goes" with a new job and apartment. What he didn't know was that Canadian tax residency isn't determined by immigration status or visas—it's determined by actions, not labels.

Within weeks of arriving, David unknowingly crossed the residency line:

- He signed a residential lease
- Opened a Canadian bank account
- Started earning income from a Canadian employer

These weren't just casual steps; they were considered *residential ties* by the Canada Revenue Agency (CRA).

David received a notice from the CRA because his Canadian tax return had not been filed for the year in which he returned and worked in Canada. CRA requests for reporting worldwide income occur **only when a return is missing or incomplete**, typically after the filing deadline (April 30th for most individuals). The realization that he had missed this requirement came as a shock.

David had assumed:

- Residency followed immigration status
- Taxes would be addressed later
- His U.S. income would remain outside Canada

None of that was true.

THE CORE RULE DAVID LEARNED TOO LATE

Canada determines tax residency based on the facts and intent—not on paperwork labels. Once an individual:

- Establishes a home
- Begins working
- Integrates financially
- Demonstrates intent to live in Canada

CRA often considers them a Canadian tax resident, even if:

- They still feel temporary
- They plan to "decide later"
- Their immigration status is time-limited

Once residency is established, Canada taxes everything, including:

- U.S. salary
- Investment income
- RSUs
- Rental income
- Retirement distributions

WHY THIS HAPPENS SO OFTEN TO AMERICANS

Americans are used to tax systems based on:

- Citizenship
- Immigration status
- Formal declarations

Canada's system, however, assumes that if your life is here, so are your taxes. David's case isn't unique—it's a common scenario.

LESSONS LEARNED

Once Canadian residency begins, every U.S. asset, account, and income stream is viewed through the Canadian tax lens. Understanding this is critical for Americans moving to Canada.

JASON AND THE PFIC DISASTER

Jason's mistake wasn't reckless. It was ordinary.

After moving from California to Toronto, Jason followed the common advice: he met with a Canadian banker, opened local accounts, and invested in what appeared to be a standard Canadian mutual fund.

From a Canadian perspective, everything was perfectly fine.

From a U.S. tax perspective, however, it was a financial landmine.

WHAT JASON WAS TOLD — AND WHAT HE WASN'T

The advice Jason received was straightforward:

- "You live in Canada now."
- "You should invest like a Canadian."
- "This is a diversified, low-cost mutual fund."

What no one explained was a rule buried deep in the U.S. tax code: the PFIC (Passive Foreign Investment Company) rules.

Under U.S. law, most Canadian mutual funds, ETFs, and pooled investments are automatically classified as PFICs when held by U.S. citizens or green card holders. PFIC rules do not apply to these investments when held inside an RRSP. This classification exposes Jason to one of the most punishing tax regimes the IRS enforces.

THE LETTER THAT CHANGED EVERYTHING

A year later, Jason's U.S. tax preparer delivered the bad news:

- A PFIC disclosure package for several Canadian mutual funds and ETFs, which could easily exceed 200 pages
- Several hundred dollars in additional U.S. tax per Form 8621 filing, depending on the number of funds held
- Specialized tax preparation fees just to calculate the damage

Jason's reaction was disbelief:

"I bought a normal mutual fund. How is this worse than crypto?"

For Americans, it's much worse.

WHY PFIC RULES ARE SO PUNITIVE

PFIC rules aim to discourage Americans from holding foreign pooled investments. The penalties are severe:

- Taxation of unrealized gains
- Interest charges may accrue in future years if PFIC reporting is not completed on time; in this example, since the mutual fund was purchased after moving to Canada, there would be no prior-year interest.
- Loss of capital-gains treatment
- Complex, time-consuming, and expensive annual reporting

Even small accounts can lead to overwhelming compliance costs. Large portfolios can become unmanageable.

Once triggered, PFIC exposure is difficult—and sometimes impossible—to undo retroactively.

WHY THIS HAPPENS SO OFTEN TO AMERICANS IN CANADA

Jason's experience is not unique. It's a common mistake

because:

- Canadian advisors are not trained in U.S. PFIC rules
- U.S. advisors often disengage once a client moves abroad
- Banks default to domestic products that are toxic for Americans

Each professional sees only half the picture.

The result is a structure that works perfectly under Canadian rules and fails catastrophically under U.S. ones.

THE LARGER LESSON

For Americans moving to Canada, "local" investing is rarely as safe as it seems.

What looks conservative and compliant in Canada can become punitive, expensive, and irreversible under U.S. tax law.

This is not a niche issue. It's one of the most costly mistakes Americans make after crossing the border.

LESSONS LEARNED

Jason's experience serves as a critical reminder that local investing can backfire when cross-border tax rules aren't properly considered. For Americans in Canada, investing locally without cross-border planning can trigger expensive and irreversible penalties.

MEGAN'S EMPLOYER STOCK EXPLODES INTO A TAX NIGHTMARE

Megan didn't change jobs when she moved to Canada.

That was part of the appeal.

Her New York–based employer approved a transfer, her role stayed the same, and her compensation package—salary, RSUs, and stock options—continued exactly as before. On paper, it looked seamless.

In practice, it was anything but.

WHEN TWO COUNTRIES TAX THE SAME PAYCHEQUE

Megan's stock compensation was governed by two different

systems that do not naturally coordinate with one another. From the U.S. perspective:

- RSUs and stock options were considered U.S.-sourced compensation.
- The U.S. taxed vesting based on where the work was performed when the equity was earned.

From the Canadian perspective:

- Megan was now a Canadian tax resident.
- Canada taxed the same RSU income as Canadian employment income.

Both countries asserted taxing rights.

Neither automatically stepped aside.

WHAT WENT WRONG

The breakdown didn't happen because the rules were unclear.

It happened because no one was looking at the full timeline. Key problems included:

- Vesting schedules that spanned pre- and post-move periods
- Incorrect sourcing of income between countries
- No coordination of foreign tax credits
- Employers issuing U.S. tax slips that didn't align with
- Canadian reporting requirements

Each accountant worked in isolation.

Each assumed the other side would "handle it."

No one did.

THE COST OF MISALIGNMENT

By the time Megan realized something was wrong:

- Both countries had already taxed the income
- Deadlines for corrective elections had passed
- Amended filings became complex and expensive

The result was a tax bill exceeding $40,000 that could largely have been avoided with proper cross-border planning.

Megan summed it up bluntly:

"Everyone said this was normal stock compensation. Nobody said it was cross-border explosives."

WHY STOCK COMPENSATION IS ESPECIALLY DANGEROUS ACROSS BORDERS

Equity compensation sits at the intersection of:

- Employment law
- Tax residency
- Income sourcing rules

- Treaty interpretation

Small errors in timing or classification cascade quickly.

Common traps include:

- RSUs taxed in the wrong country first
- Options exercised without understanding residency impact
- Missing treaty relief elections
- Employers reporting income inconsistently across jurisdictions

Once filings are made incorrectly, fixing them often requires years of amended returns.

THE CORE LESSON

Stock compensation does not move cleanly across borders.

It must be:

- Re-mapped
- Re-sourced
- Re-reported
- And re-coordinated

Assuming it will "sort itself out" is one of the most expensive assumptions an American can make when moving to Canada.

THE LIFE INSURANCE THAT STOPPED WORKING THE MOMENT THEY LANDED

Jake had done what many financially disciplined Americans do long before any international move.

He had purchased a U.S. whole-life insurance policy designed to provide permanent coverage, tax-advantaged growth, and estate protection for his family.

When he relocated from Texas to Calgary, he assumed the policy would simply continue in the background.

It didn't.

WHY LIFE INSURANCE DOES NOT TRAVEL WELL

Life insurance is governed by domestic tax rules, not by portability.

When Jake became a Canadian tax resident, his policy didn't change—but the rules surrounding it did.

Under Canadian tax law, many U.S. life insurance structures no longer receive the same treatment they enjoyed in the United States.

What was once efficient became problematic almost overnight.

WHAT CHANGED AFTER ENTRY INTO CANADA

Once Canadian residency applied, Jake discovered that:

- Tax-sheltered growth rules no longer aligned
- Canada calculates exempt policy status differently than the U.S., often reducing or eliminating tax-deferred growth.
- Policy loans became taxable events
- Loans taken against the policy—previously considered tax-free access—were now potentially taxable in Canada.
- Cost basis calculations changed
- Adjusted cost basis under Canadian rules did not match U.S. calculations, creating unexpected taxable gains.
- Beneficiary and estate treatment shifted
- The policy no longer fit cleanly into Canadian estate planning assumptions.

None of these issues were visible at the border. They surfaced months later—usually when an accountant finally reviewed the policy in detail.

WHY THIS CATCHES AMERICANS OFF GUARD

In the U.S., life insurance is often treated as a stable, long-term planning pillar.

It is rarely revisited unless a major life event occurs.

Moving countries is a major life event—but most people don't think of insurance as something that needs immigration planning.

That assumption is costly.

THE HIDDEN RISK: DEFERRED PROBLEMS BECOME IMMEDIATE

Many returning or relocating individuals do nothing with their

U.S. policies for years.

The danger is not immediate cancellation—it's silent erosion.

Over time:

- Loans compound into taxable exposure
- Growth loses its sheltered status
- Estate plans unravel
- Policy exits become punitive

By the time action is taken, options are limited.

THE CORE LESSON

Life insurance is not internationally neutral.

A policy optimized for one country can become inefficient—or outright damaging—under another country's tax system.

For Americans moving to Canada, insurance must be:

- Reviewed
- Reclassified
- And, in some cases, replaced

Assuming coverage will "just keep working" is one of the most

common—and expensive—mistakes in cross-border moves.

In the next section, we'll step away from tax forms and policies and look at something far more personal: the cost-of-living shock many Americans never see coming.

THE COST OF LIVING SHOCK — "WE WEREN'T READY FOR THIS."

Daniel and Megan had done their homework—or so they thought.

They expected colder winters.

They expected different cultural norms.

They expected a smaller living space.

What they did not expect was how quickly everyday costs in Canada would overwhelm assumptions formed in the United States.

WHY THE COST SHOCK FEELS SO SUDDEN

For many Americans, the move to Canada is framed emotionally: safety, healthcare access, quality of life. What often gets underestimated is that Canada's social systems are funded very differently—and that difference shows up in daily expenses.

Daniel put it bluntly after their first year in Vancouver:

"We came from Manhattan... and Vancouver still shocked us."

THE EXPENSES AMERICANS RARELY ANTICIPATE

Americans are often surprised by how quickly costs stack up across categories they assumed would be similar or cheaper.

Common shock points include:

- Mobile and internet services
- Plans that cost $60–$80 in the U.S. routinely exceed
- $120 per month in Canada, with fewer data allowances.
- Groceries and household goods
- Food prices are often 20–40% higher, especially for imported or specialty items.
- Alcohol and entertainment
- Provincial taxation and regulation make alcohol, dining out, and events significantly more expensive.
- Childcare and education costs
- In major cities, daycare fees can rival mortgage payments.
- Housing and real estate
- Vancouver and Toronto pricing often surprises even Americans from New York, California, or Seattle.

- Combined federal and provincial taxes
- Marginal tax rates exceeding 50% are a shock to those accustomed to lower combined U.S. rates.

WHY THIS HITS NEW RESIDENTS HARDER

In the U.S., many costs are fragmented—healthcare through employers, education through local districts, taxes spread across multiple layers.

In Canada, the funding model is more centralized and visible. For new residents:

- Paychecks feel smaller faster
- Discretionary spending tightens sooner
- Long-term savings projections change

This adjustment often coincides with:

- Higher income tax withholding
- Currency conversion losses
- Ongoing U.S. compliance costs

The result is a sense that expenses increased from every direction at once.

THE PSYCHOLOGICAL IMPACT

The cost-of-living shock is not just financial—it's emotional.

Many Americans experience:

- Guilt for feeling financially strained in a "safer" system
- Stress when savings don't stretch as expected
- Frustration when comparisons to U.S. life no longer hold

This isn't a failure of planning.

It's a failure of *expectation* setting.

THE CORE LESSON

Moving to Canada often improves predictability—but at a higher baseline cost.

Understanding that reality early allows families to:

- Adjust lifestyle expectations
- Rebuild budgets accurately
- Avoid compounding stress during the transition period

In the next section, we'll examine a technical requirement many Americans overlook entirely—foreign asset reporting—and why it begins the moment Canadian accounts are opened.

THE FOREIGN ASSET FILING THEY DIDN'T KNOW ABOUT

Daniel thought the hardest compliance work was behind him once he started filing Canadian tax returns. He was wrong.

The first real shock came not from CRA—but from the IRS.

HOW THE PROBLEM BEGINS

The moment Daniel and Megan opened everyday Canadian accounts, they unknowingly crossed a U.S. reporting threshold.

Not an income threshold. Not an investment threshold.

A disclosure threshold.

For U.S. citizens and green card holders, foreign reporting obligations begin the instant total non-U.S. financial accounts exceed $10,000 USD at any point during the year.

Not per account. Not on December 31. At *any time.*

Daniel crossed that line within weeks.

WHAT TRIGGERED THE FILINGS

The triggers were ordinary, practical steps of settling into Canada:

- Opening a Canadian chequing account for payroll
- Opening a savings account for expenses
- Receiving RSU income into a Canadian account
- Holding employer stock or cash temporarily

Individually, none of these seemed significant.

Together, they created a reporting obligation Daniel didn't know existed.

THE FORMS NO ONE WARNED THEM ABOUT

Once the threshold was crossed, Daniel was required to file the forms in the following year along with his U.S. tax returns:

- FBAR (FinCEN Form 114)
- Reports all foreign accounts once aggregate balances exceed $10,000 USD.
- FATCA Form 8938
- Additional reporting attached to the U.S. tax return when asset values exceed higher thresholds.

These filings are not optional, even when:

- All income is properly taxed
- No tax is owed to the U.S.
- Accounts are ordinary personal banking accounts

WHY THIS IS SO COMMONLY MISSED

Most Canadian accountants do not handle U.S. compliance. Most U.S. accountants assume foreign accounts are minimal or temporary.

Daniel was stuck in the gap.

Neither professional flagged the issue until a review uncovered missing disclosures—two years late.

THE PENALTIES CATCH PEOPLE OFF GUARD

FBAR penalties are not proportional to harm. They are statutory.

- Non-willful penalties can reach $16,536 per year, per account
- Willful penalties are far higher
- Penalties apply even when no tax is owed

Daniel's reaction was disbelief:

"These were normal bank accounts. Not offshore shelters." The IRS makes no such distinction.

WHY TIMING MAKES THIS WORSE

Foreign reporting obligations can feel urgent early in the move, before most Americans feel settled:

- Before budgets stabilize
- Before advisors are aligned
- Before systems are fully rebuilt

However, it is important to note that the filing of FBAR and FATCA forms is not immediate. You have until the following year to submit these forms along with your U.S. tax return, so the apparent urgency arises from managing multiple transitions simultaneously, not from an immediate filing requirement.

That is why mistakes can compound quickly if planning is delayed.

THE STRUCTURAL RISK

This is not about wrongdoing. It is about visibility.

Once accounts exist:

- They appear in financial records
- They intersect with employer reporting
- They create audit trails across borders

Fixing missed filings is possible—but expensive, stressful, and time-consuming.

THE CORE LESSON

For Americans moving to Canada, foreign reporting is not a niche issue.

It is a default requirement of everyday life. Understanding this early allows individuals to:

- File correctly from the start
- Avoid penalty exposure
- Coordinate U.S. and Canadian advisors properly

In the next section, we'll look at what happens when these pressures accumulate—and how quickly a cross-border life can begin to unravel without coordinated guidance.

HOW EVERYTHING BEGAN UNRAVELING

By their second year in Canada, Daniel and Megan no longer felt like newcomers. They had jobs, routines, and social lives. On the surface, the move looked successful.

Financially, however, the strain was becoming impossible to ignore.

What made the situation so destabilizing wasn't a single mistake. It was how multiple small, uncoordinated issues began reinforcing one another.

The Compounding Effect

Each decision made sense in isolation:

- A Canadian advisor recommended local investments
- A U.S. advisor restricted accounts after an address change
- An employer continued issuing RSUs under U.S. payroll
- Currency was converted as needed through major banks
- Insurance policies were left unchanged

None of these choices felt reckless.

Together, they created a system that no longer worked.

WHERE THE BREAKDOWN OCCURRED

By mid–year two, the following problems surfaced almost simultaneously:

- U.S. brokerage accounts were frozen once the Canadian address was updated
- Canadian investments triggered PFIC exposure for U.S. filings
- RSUs were taxed incorrectly in both countries
- U.S. returns were filed late, while Canadian residency was questioned
- Foreign reporting penalties began accumulating
- Currency conversion losses quietly eroded capital

- Insurance structures no longer behaved as expected under Canadian rules

Each issue fed the next. Fixing one revealed another. Megan described the feeling precisely:

"It felt like we crossed the border and triggered two tax systems at the same time."

That is exactly what had happened.

WHY THIS HAPPENS SO OFTEN

Cross-border failures rarely come from ignorance. They come from fragmentation.

- One professional sees only the U.S. side
- Another sees only Canada
- Neither is responsible for integration

In domestic planning, that approach often works. In cross-border transitions, it fails.

No single advisor flagged how one action would affect the other system.

THE FALSE SENSE OF PROGRESS

Daniel and Megan were doing everything they believed was responsible:

- Filing taxes
- Using licensed advisors
- Disclosing information
- Following instructions

However, the structure they were relying on was flawed. Compliance alone didn't guarantee success.

Despite all efforts, the system itself was fragmented—each advisor handled only one side of the equation, and no one coordinated the whole picture.

What seemed like responsible planning ended up being insufficient because no one was addressing both U.S. and Canadian systems together.

THE TURNING POINT

The breaking point wasn't financial—it was emotional. Daniel said:

"We weren't afraid of taxes anymore. We were afraid of making another move."

Every decision felt risky:

- Transfer funds or wait?
- Sell assets or hold?
- Change advisors or stay put?

When uncertainty becomes constant, momentum stops.

THE UNDERLYING ISSUE

The core problem wasn't complexity—it was misalignment between U.S. and Canadian systems.

Each system operated independently, and Daniel and Megan were living in both simultaneously.

Without a unified strategy, each country's rules triggered friction, causing financial and emotional stress.

WHEN THEY FINALLY FOUND CROSS-BORDER HELP

By the time Daniel and Megan reached out for specialized guidance, they were not looking for optimization. They were looking for stability.

What they found was not a single advisor, but a coordinated cross-border framework—one that treated their life as a single system rather than two disconnected jurisdictions.

WHAT CHANGED IMMEDIATELY

The first shift was diagnostic, not tactical.

Instead of starting with tax returns or investment products, the cross-border team began by mapping Daniel and Megan's full reality:

- Immigration status and residency facts
- U.S. citizenship obligations
- Canadian tax residency triggers
- Employer compensation structure
- Existing U.S. and Canadian accounts
- Insurance contracts
- Reporting exposure on both sides

Only once the full picture was visible did solutions make sense.

REBUILDING THE FINANCIAL STRUCTURE

With clarity in place, the work became corrective and preventative:

- Restructuring investment holdings to eliminate PFIC exposure while staying suitable for Canadian residency.
- Correcting RSU taxation with treaty-based allocation between the U.S. and Canada.
- Bringing late and missing U.S. filings back into compliance.
- Coordinating FBAR and FATCA disclosures with Canadian reporting.
- Resolving U.S. brokerage account issues, including address and access problems.
- Adjusting insurance policies to align with Canadian tax treatment.
- Redesigning currency management to avoid unnecessary conversion losses.

These fixes were not isolated actions—they were part of a comprehensive, integrated strategy that addressed issues across both systems.

WHY THIS WORKED WHEN OTHERS DIDN'T

The difference was not intelligence or effort. It was licensing and scope.

Cross-border advisors operate under both regulatory frameworks. They are trained to anticipate how one country's rules will trigger consequences in the other.

Domestic advisors are rarely positioned to do this, no matter how competent they are within their own system.

Daniel put it simply:

"For the first time, someone understood both sides of our life."

FROM REACTION TO STRATEGY

Once the immediate fires were out, planning shifted forward:

- Retirement projections were rebuilt using after-tax figures from both countries.
- Reporting obligations were scheduled rather than rushed.
- Investment decisions were filtered through treaty implications.
- Currency exposure was managed proactively.
- Future relocation flexibility was preserved.

With clarity in place, the financial structure began to feel stable and structured, rather than fragile.

THE REAL VALUE OF INTEGRATED ADVICE

The goal was never perfection, but coherence.

When tax, immigration, investing, reporting, and insurance operate in harmony, decisions regain momentum, and confidence returns.

Without integrated advice, even the best intentions can unravel.

WHAT THIS SECTION TEACHES

Americans moving to Canada do not need more rules. They need one integrated map.

Without it, even well-intentioned planning unravels. With it, complexity becomes manageable.

This is the point where most cross-border stories finally turn—not because the systems became simpler, but because someone learned how to make them work together.

AMERICANS MOVING TO CANADA NEED A GUIDE, NOT A GUESS

Daniel and Megan's experience is not unusual. It is representative.

Americans moving to Canada do not fail because they ignore rules. They fail because they are subject to two complete systems at the same time, each with its own definitions, penalties, and blind spots.

What makes this transition especially dangerous is that the risks do not announce themselves immediately. They surface gradually, through frozen accounts, unexpected tax bills, duplicate reporting, and decisions that cannot be undone.

By the time most people realize something is wrong, several years have already passed.

WHAT THIS CHAPTER HAS SHOWN

Moving from the United States to Canada triggers:

- Canadian tax residency based on facts, not immigration labels
- Lifetime U.S. tax filing obligations, regardless of where you live
- Punitive PFIC rules on ordinary Canadian investments
- Double taxation risks on RSUs, stock options, and deferred compensation
- Insurance failures when U.S. policies cross into Canadian tax law
- Frozen or restricted U.S. brokerage accounts after address changes
- Immediate foreign reporting obligations the moment Canadian accounts are opened
- Compounding errors when advice is fragmented rather than integrated

None of these issues are theoretical. Every one of them appears in real cases.

WHY GUESSING FAILS

Most Americans assume that careful disclosure and good intentions will protect them. Unfortunately, neither tax system rewards assumptions.

What fails most often is not compliance, but coordination.

When each professional sees only one side of the border, no one sees the whole structure.

THE CORE LESSON

Moving countries is emotional. Managing two tax systems is technical.

Trying to do both without cross-border coordination creates unnecessary risk.

This chapter exists so the next person does not have to learn these lessons through penalties, restrictions, and stress.

THE MOVING FROM THE U.S. TO CANADA STARTER KIT

When Daniel and Megan finally understood the framework, five principles became clear.

1. RESIDENCY IS FINANCIAL, NOT EMOTIONAL

You live in Canada.

Canada taxes worldwide income.

The U.S. still taxes you because you are American.

Understanding this reality is the foundation of every correct decision that follows.

2. YOUR INVESTMENTS CANNOT CROSS THE BORDER ALONE
   - U.S. funds become restricted
   - Canadian funds become PFICs
   - RSUs and stock options can be taxed twice A portfolio must be rebuilt, not transferred blindly.
3. THE IRS DOES NOT LET GO

Moving north does not end:

- U.S. tax returns
- FBAR filings
- FATCA disclosures

- Form 8938
- Pension and retirement reporting

These obligations continue for life unless U.S. citizenship changes.

4. CURRENCY DECISIONS MATTER MORE THAN PEOPLE EXPECT

Hidden FX spreads quietly destroy capital.

Large conversions without strategy cost thousands. Currency planning is part of wealth preservation.

5. INSURANCE DOES NOT TRAVEL WELL

Life insurance, health structures, and policy taxation change immediately at the border.

Assuming continuity is one of the most expensive mistakes Americans make.

FINAL THOUGHT

Americans moving to Canada do not need to be warned away from the opportunity. They need to be properly prepared for it.

With informed planning, coordinated advice, and an integrated framework, the move north can be exactly what people hoped for.

Without it, even a well-intentioned relocation can unravel.

CHAPTER 5
CROSS-BORDER REAL ESTATE: SELLING U.S. PROPERTY & BUYING IN CANADA

In This Chapter, You Will Learn...

In this chapter, you will learn why selling U.S. real estate and purchasing property in Canada is one of the most complex—and most misunderstood—cross-border financial events.

Specifically, this chapter explains:

- Why Canadians and returning Canadians are treated as foreign sellers under U.S. law, even after years of living and working in the United States
- How FIRPTA withholding works, why 15% is taken at closing, and what must be done to recover excess amounts
- How Canada taxes the sale of U.S. property as worldwide income, including the impact of currency conversion on capital gains
- Why state taxes may still apply long after you believe you've left the U.S. system
- How currency conversion spreads quietly erase tens of thousands of dollars during property sales
- What surprises Americans and returning Canadians face when buying property in Canada, including lending rules, credit recognition, and stress tests
- How GST/HST, renovations, and principal residence rules introduce new risks after returning home
- Why gains that are tax-free in the U.S. can become fully taxable in Canada
- How timing mismatches between IRS and CRA systems create cash-flow and reporting challenges

- Why cross-border real estate must be treated as a financial migration, not a simple transaction

This chapter provides the framework readers need to understand how real estate crosses the border—and why proper coordination before selling or buying is essential to protecting wealth, avoiding unnecessary tax, and preventing irreversible mistakes.

UNDERSTANDING FIRPTA: WHY CANADIANS ARE TREATED AS "FOREIGN SELLERS" IN THE U.S.

One of the biggest surprises for Canadians selling U.S. real estate is that they are treated as foreign sellers by the IRS—even if they lived, worked, and owned property in the U.S. for decades.

The key issue is the taxpayer's U.S. status at the time of sale, not merely Canadian tax residency. FIRPTA—the Foreign Investment in Real Property Tax Act—applies to non-U.S. persons, meaning individuals who are not U.S. citizens or green card holders.

If the taxpayer is a non-U.S. person and a non-resident of the U.S., FIRPTA withholding applies regardless of Canadian residency. FIRPTA also applies to non-U.S. persons who are residents of countries other than Canada.

WHAT FIRPTA ACTUALLY DOES

FIRPTA requires that 15% of the gross sale price be withheld by the buyer or escrow agent at the time of closing.

This withholding is sent directly to the IRS, regardless of:

- Whether a gain was made.
- Whether the gain is small or even nonexistent.
- Whether you ultimately owe little or no U.S. tax.

Exclusions and reductions:

- No withholding is required if the property is sold for less than USD $300,000 and the buyer intends to use it as a principal residence.

- In some cases, withholding can be reduced from 15% to 10% if certain conditions are met.

This amount is a **prepayment** and not the final tax bill. To recover any excess withholding, sellers must take specific steps **before closing**.

WHY THIS FEELS SO WRONG TO SELLERS

Paul and Marissa were shocked because, in their minds:

- They were Canadians returning home.
- The house was their former residence.
- The sale felt like a normal life transition.

But FIRPTA doesn't account for:

- Intentions.
- History in the U.S.
- Whether the property was once their home.

The rule applies mechanically—if you're a non-U.S. tax resident and non-U.S. citizen or green card holder at the time of sale, FIRPTA applies.

WHAT YOU MUST DO TO RECOVER FIRPTA WITHHOLDING

To recover the FIRPTA withholding, sellers must:

- File a U.S. non-resident tax return (Form 1040-NR).
- Often file a state tax return, depending on location.
- Calculate actual U.S. capital gains tax.
- Claim the FIRPTA withholding as a credit.
- Apply for reduced withholding using Form 8288-B before closing (if applicable).
- Wait months for IRS processing and refunds.

Without proper planning, sellers may have six figures withheld at closing, even if the final tax owed is far lower.

WHERE MANY CANADIANS GO WRONG

Common mistakes Canadians make when selling U.S. property include:

- Learning about FIRPTA only after closing.
- Assuming citizenship overrides residency.
- Failing to apply for a withholding reduction in advance.
- Not coordinating U.S. and Canadian tax reporting.
- Treating FIRPTA as a penalty instead of a prepayment.

These mistakes can result in significant financial setbacks, often making an already complex process even more difficult to navigate.

KEY REALITY CHECK

FIRPTA is not optional. It is not discretionary.

And it is not intuitive.

It is the starting point for every cross-border real estate sale involving U.S. property and Canadian residents who are not U.S. persons.

In the next section, we'll look at what happens after the U.S. side is handled — and why Canada's tax treatment often creates a second, unexpected layer of tax exposure.

CANADIAN TAX ON THE SALE OF U.S. PROPERTY

Once the U.S. side of the sale is addressed, many Canadians assume the hardest part is over. However, Canada taxes its residents on worldwide income, which includes capital gains from U.S. real estate.

The fact that the property is located outside Canada doesn't reduce the Canada Revenue Agency's (CRA) claim once Canadian residency is re-established.

WHAT CANADA REQUIRES YOU TO REPORT

If you are a Canadian tax resident at the time of sale, you must:

- Report the capital gain on your Canadian return
- Calculate the gain in Canadian dollars, using a stepped-up cost basis equal to the fair market value (FMV) of the property on the date you

became a Canadian resident. This may reduce Canadian capital gains compared with U.S. tax liability.Disclose the disposition as foreign property

- Claim a foreign tax credit only for the final U.S. federal and state tax liability, not for FIRPTA withholding, since a portion of FIRPTA may be refundable after filing

This reporting is mandatory even if:

- You already paid tax to the IRS
- The U.S. treated part of the gain as tax-exempt
- The sale felt like a clean exit from U.S. life

CRA's system operates independently of the U.S. system.

THE CURRENCY CONVERSION TRAP

Currency conversion is a hidden factor that can affect the financial outcome of a U.S. property sale.

When U.S. property is sold, proceeds are received in U.S. dollars. Once those funds are converted to Canadian dollars, exchange rates and conversion spreads come into play, impacting the final outcome—even though they don't appear on a tax return.

Two risks are involved:

- Exchange rate movement between the purchase and sale.
- Conversion spreads applied by financial institutions.

Both can erode the final result significantly.

FOREIGN TAX CREDITS ARE NOT AUTOMATIC

While Canada offers a foreign tax credit for taxes paid to the U.S., it's not a straightforward, dollar-for-dollar match.

Common issues that arise include:

- Timing mismatches between U.S. and Canadian filings.
- FIRPTA withholding exceeding the actual U.S. tax owed.
- Limited credits based on Canadian marginal tax rates.

- Delays in U.S. refunds affecting Canadian tax filings.

Without proper coordination, sellers can overpay or underreport tax obligations.

SECONDARY EFFECTS MANY DON'T EXPECT

Reporting a large capital gain in Canada can trigger consequences beyond income tax, including:

- OAS clawback (for retirees).
- Movement into higher tax brackets.
- Loss of income-tested benefits.
- Increased scrutiny on foreign asset reporting.

None of these outcomes are automatically flagged; they become apparent only after filing.

WHY THIS CATCHES SO MANY PEOPLE

Paul and Marissa's experience is typical. They assumed:

- Paying U.S. tax first settled the issue
- Canada would "net it out" cleanly
- The systems would talk to each other They don't.

THE CORE TAKEAWAY

Selling U.S. property as a Canadian resident and non-U.S. person creates two parallel tax calculations, not one:

- A U.S. calculation governed by FIRPTA and IRS rules
- A Canadian calculation governed by worldwide income and currency rules

Managing one without planning for the other is where costly surprises occur.

In the next section, we'll examine how state taxes add a third layer of complexity—and why the state where the property is located matters just as much as the country.

STATE TAXES STILL APPLY

Even after moving back to Canada, state tax obligations may still apply.

U.S. real estate is taxed not only at the federal level but also at the state level, where each state has its own rules. The state where the property is located may assert the right to tax:

- Capital gains on the sale.
- Rental income earned prior to the sale.
- Depreciation recapture.
- Additional withholding at closing.

This applies even if you no longer live in the state or are filing as a non-resident for federal purposes. From the state's perspective, the property itself creates the tax connection.

WHY STATE TAXES MATTER

When you sell U.S. property, the state where the property is located may assert the right to tax:

- Capital gains on the sale
- Rental income earned prior to sale
- Depreciation recapture
- Additional withholding at closing

This applies even if:

- You no longer live in the state
- You are no longer a U.S. resident
- You are filing as a non-resident for federal purposes

From the state's perspective, the property itself creates the tax connection.

STATES THAT COMMONLY AFFECT SNOWBIRDS AND RETURNEES

Different states handle real estate sales very differently:

- California

- Aggressive enforcement, complex residency rules, and state capital gains tax. California is not bound by the Canada–U.S. tax treaty in the same way the IRS is, which limits relief options.
- Arizona
- State tax applies to gains and depreciation recapture, with required non-resident filings even after departure.
- Hawaii
- Often imposes state withholding on real estate sales, adding another layer of cash-flow strain.
- Florida, Texas, Washington
- No state income tax, which simplifies the sale considerably. However, federal and Canadian obligations still remain.

RESIDENCY ARGUMENTS DON'T ALWAYS PROTECT YOU

Some sellers assume they can avoid state tax by arguing they were no longer residents. In real estate sales, this argument rarely succeeds.

States focus on:

- Where the property is located
- Where income was generated
- Whether filings are required under state law

Residency disputes tend to matter more for ongoing income than for property dispositions.

WITHHOLDING, FILING, AND REFUND DELAYS

In some states:

- Tax is withheld at closing
- Funds are remitted before final tax is calculated
- Refunds require filing a state return
- Processing times can stretch for months

This creates timing problems when:

- Canadian tax is due before U.S. refunds arrive
- Foreign tax credits depend on finalized U.S. numbers

WHY STATE TAX PLANNING IS OFTEN MISSED

Many Canadian accountants are unfamiliar with U.S. state rules. Many U.S. preparers stop at the federal level. The gap sits squarely in the middle.

Paul and Marissa's confusion was not unusual. Their federal filing was addressed, but state obligations emerged later, forcing amended returns and additional professional fees.

THE PRACTICAL REALITY

Selling U.S. property often involves three tax systems, not two:

- U.S. federal tax
- U.S. state tax
- Canadian tax

Each one has its own timelines, definitions, and paperwork.

THE CORE TAKEAWAY

State taxes can materially change the economics of a U.S. property sale. Ignoring them does not eliminate the obligation—it simply delays the discovery.

In the next section, we'll look at how currency conversion quietly magnifies tax and cash-flow losses, even when every filing is technically correct.

CURRENCY CONVERSION TRAPS

Currency conversion is rarely treated as a planning decision. Most people see it as a mechanical step that happens after the sale, handled by whatever institution is holding the funds. In cross-border real estate transactions, that assumption can quietly erase tens of thousands of dollars.

Paul and Marissa experienced this firsthand.

WHY CURRENCY BECOMES A TAX ISSUE

When U.S. property is sold, proceeds are received in U.S. dollars. The moment those funds are converted into Canadian dollars, exchange rates and spreads become part of the financial outcome, even though they never appear on a tax return.

Two separate risks exist:

- Exchange rate movement between purchase and sale
- Conversion spreads charged by financial institutions

Both can materially change the net result.

THE HIDDEN COST OF BANK CONVERSIONS

Most Canadian banks apply a spread of approximately 2.5% to 3.5% on large currency conversions. This spread is rarely disclosed clearly. It is embedded in the rate offered.

In Paul and Marissa's case:

- Sale proceeds: USD $740,000
- Bank spread: approximately 3%
- Immediate cost: over $22,000

No tax form recorded this loss. No statement highlighted it. It simply disappeared in the exchange rate.

WHY THIS MATTERS FOR CANADIAN TAX REPORTING

Currency conversion also affects Canadian tax calculations.

For CRA purposes:

- Capital gains are calculated in Canadian dollars
- Exchange rates at purchase and sale both matter
- The timing of conversion can influence reported income

A poorly timed conversion can:

- Increase reported capital gains
- Push income into higher marginal brackets
- Trigger OAS clawback
- Create cash-flow strain before refunds arrive

BETTER ALTERNATIVES EXIST

Specialized foreign exchange providers typically offer:

- Transparent pricing

- Spreads closer to 0.20%–1.0%
- Better documentation for large transfers
- Faster settlement and flexibility

For large transactions, the difference between a retail bank rate and a specialist rate can exceed the cost of professional tax advice.

WHY PEOPLE MISS THIS STEP

Currency conversion feels operational, not strategic. By the time the issue is noticed, the conversion has already happened.

Paul's reaction was common:

"We spent months planning the sale... and lost more on the exchange than on legal fees."

THE CORE TAKEAWAY

Currency decisions should be treated as part of the transaction—not as an afterthought.

In cross-border real estate sales:

- Exchange rates affect taxable outcomes
- Spreads affect real wealth
- Timing affects cash flow

Handled correctly, currency conversion protects value. Handled casually, it quietly erodes it.

In the next section, we'll turn to what happens after the sale, when Canadians and Americans attempt to buy property in Canada—and why that transition is rarely as smooth as expected.

BUYING A HOME IN CANADA AFTER SELLING IN THE U.S.

Many Canadians and Americans assume that once a U.S. property is sold, purchasing a home in Canada will be familiar territory. The reality is very different. Canadian real estate financing, tax treatment, and regulatory requirements operate under a far more conservative framework, and the transition often exposes gaps that sellers did not anticipate.

Paul and Marissa discovered that selling in the U.S. was only half the transaction. Buying in Canada introduced a new set of hurdles.

CANADIAN MORTGAGE RULES ARE NOT U.S. RULES

Canadian lenders assess borrowers differently than U.S. banks.

Key differences include:

- More conservative lending standards
- Mandatory application of the mortgage stress test
- Stricter income verification
- Limited recognition of U.S. credit history
- Heavier documentation requirements for cross-border income

Even buyers with substantial equity from a U.S. sale can face delays or denials if documentation is incomplete.

U.S. CREDIT DOES NOT FULLY TRANSFER

Many returnees are surprised to learn that:

- U.S. credit scores are not directly portable
- Canadian lenders rely on Canadian credit files
- Newly returned residents may appear "thin-file" or inactive

This can affect:

- Mortgage approvals
- Interest rates
- Required down payments

Rebuilding Canadian credit often takes time, even for financially strong buyers.

DOWN PAYMENTS CREATE THEIR OWN COMPLICATIONS

Funds held in U.S. accounts may:

- Require conversion into CAD

- Need source-of-funds documentation
- Trigger compliance checks
- Be delayed by frozen brokerage or banking restrictions

Timing matters. If funds are not accessible when an offer closes, buyers can lose properties or deposits.

TAX AND REGULATORY SURPRISES

Buyers may encounter:

- GST/HST on new builds
- Complex rebate eligibility rules
- Foreign buyer restrictions in certain provinces
- A federal foreign buyer ban for non-Canadian citizens who are not permanent residents and do not hold a valid work visa
- Provincial property transfer taxes that differ significantly from U.S. norms

Misunderstanding these rules can increase the total acquisition cost substantially, especially for U.S. individuals who move to Canada to retire and do not yet have Canadian status.

WHY THIS FEELS SO DISRUPTIVE

Paul and Marissa expected the purchase to feel like a continuation of their previous life. Instead, it felt like starting over.

They learned that:

- Canadian lenders required Canadian tax returns
- U.S. account statements were not always accepted
- Their advisors were not aligned across borders

THE CORE TAKEAWAY

Selling U.S. property does not automatically prepare you to buy in Canada.

The purchase side introduces:

- New lending standards
- New tax considerations

- New compliance expectations

Without preparation, even well-funded buyers can encounter unnecessary friction.

In the next section, we'll look at renovations, new builds, and GST/HST rules, and why post-purchase decisions can create additional tax exposure if handled casually.

RENOVATIONS, CAPITAL GAINS, AND GST/HST RULES

For many returning Canadians and new arrivals, buying a home is only the beginning. Renovations, additions, or even new construction often follow soon after. What surprises many is that Canadian tax rules treat these post-purchase decisions far more formally than the U.S. system, and small missteps can have outsized consequences.

Paul and Marissa nearly learned this the hard way.

RENOVATIONS ARE NOT JUST LIFESTYLE DECISIONS

In Canada, renovations can affect:

- Principal residence status
- Capital gains calculations
- Eligibility for GST/HST rebates
- Audit exposure years later

What feels like a straightforward improvement project can quietly become a tax issue.

GST/HST ON NEW BUILDS AND MAJOR RENOVATIONS

Canada applies GST/HST differently depending on the nature of the project.

Key points many buyers miss:

- Newly built homes and substantially renovated homes may be subject to GST/HST

- Rebates exist, but they are:
    - Time-sensitive
    - Documentation-heavy
    - Easy to lose through technical errors
- Occupancy dates matter
- Filing deadlines are strict

Paul and Marissa almost lost a rebate simply because receipts were incomplete and filing was delayed.

PRINCIPAL RESIDENCE TIMING MATTERS

Canada's principal residence exemption is generous, but it is not automatic.

Issues arise when:

- The home is not occupied immediately
- Renovations delay move-in
- Portions of the property are rented
- Multiple properties are owned during the same period CRA looks at use, intent, and timing, not just ownership.

RENOVATION COSTS AND CAPITAL GAINS

Proper documentation is essential. Renovation costs may:

- Increase adjusted cost base
- Reduce future capital gains
- Support rebate claims

Without records, CRA may disallow claims entirely, even if the work clearly occurred.

WHY THIS FEELS UNFORGIVING

The U.S. system often allows more flexibility and informal documentation. Canada does not.

Canadian rules assume:

- Careful recordkeeping
- Strict timelines

- Clear classification of use

Paul summed it up bluntly:

"We weren't doing anything aggressive. We just didn't know the rules were this precise."

THE CORE TAKEAWAY

Renovations in Canada carry tax consequences that extend far beyond construction costs.

Handled properly, they:

- Preserve principal residence protection
- Secure GST/HST rebates
- Reduce future capital gains

Handled casually, they:

- Trigger lost rebates
- Increase taxable gains
- Invite audit attention

In the next section, we'll examine one of the most frustrating surprises of all: why Canada taxes gains that the U.S. exempts, and how two reasonable systems can produce conflicting outcomes on the same property.

THE FINAL SURPRISE: CANADA TAXES WHAT THE U.S. DOESN'T

For many Canadians and Americans returning to Canada, the most frustrating surprise is the difference in tax treatment of housing gains between the U.S. and Canada.

Paul and Marissa assumed that because the U.S. treated their home as a principal residence with tax exemptions, Canada would follow the same logic.

However, Canada may allow you to claim the Principal Residence Exemption (PRE) on a foreign property, provided you were a Canadian resident and meet the PRE guidelines.

In the U.S.:

- Up to $250,000 of gain (single) or $500,000 (married) on a principal residence can be excluded from federal tax.
- This exemption applies even if the home is located outside the U.S. and sold after years of U.S. residency.

In Canada:

- The PRE generally applies only to Canadian properties, but a property located outside Canada may qualify as your principal residence for a particular year if you were a Canadian resident during that year and the property meets the PRE criteria.
- If you acquire a foreign property after becoming a Canadian resident, CRA normally deems you to acquire the property at fair market value at that time, so any unrealized gain before residency is generally not taxable in Canada.
- Gains on U.S. real estate are fully taxable in Canada once Canadian tax residency is established.

Two Countries, Two Completely Different Philosophies

The U.S. and Canada approach housing gains from fundamentally different perspectives:

In the United States:

- Up to $250,000 (single) or $500,000 (married) of gain can be excluded on a principal residence.
- Many long-term homeowners pay little or no federal tax on the sale.

In Canada:

- Foreign properties do not qualify for the principal residence exemption, even if they were your primary home.

Paul summed it up simply:

"How can the same house be tax-free there and taxable here?" The answer is clear:

Canada taxes worldwide gains of its residents, without carving out foreign housing exemptions.

WHY THIS CATCHES PEOPLE OFF GUARD

Most people assume tax systems will "line up" through treaties. They rarely do.

The Canada–U.S. tax treaty:

- Prevents double taxation in many cases
- Allows foreign tax credits
- Does not force Canada to adopt U.S. housing exemptions

So even if:

- The U.S. owes nothing on the sale, and
- FIRPTA withholding is later refunded,

Canada may still assess a significant capital gains tax.

THE COMPOUNDING EFFECT

This mismatch often creates secondary consequences:

- Higher marginal tax rates in the year of sale
- OAS clawbacks for retirees
- Loss of income-tested benefits
- Surprise instalment requirements for future years

Because the U.S. doesn't warn sellers—and CRA doesn't either—many people discover this only after the fact.

WHAT COULD HAVE HELPED

With planning, some exposure can be reduced or timed better:

- Coordinating the sale date with Canadian residency timing
- Using capital losses strategically
- Work with a cross-border tax accountant
- Managing income stacking in the year of sale
- Planning currency conversion carefully

Without planning, the outcome feels arbitrary and punitive.

THE REALITY

Neither country is "wrong."

They are simply applying their own tax rules.

When a property is owned by a Canadian resident but subject to U.S. and Canadian tax rules, differences in timing, reporting, and filing requirements can create practical challenges—even if both systems are similarly strict.

WHERE THIS LEAVES YOU

By the time a U.S. property is sold and a Canadian home is purchased, individuals are often dealing with:

- FIRPTA withholding
- U.S. federal and state filings
- Canadian capital gains tax
- Currency conversion losses
- Mortgage qualification stress
- Benefit clawbacks

This is why cross-border real estate is not just a transaction—it is a multi-system financial event.

In the concluding section, we'll pull these threads together and explain why real estate is often the most misunderstood—and most expensive—cross-border move of all, and how proper planning changes the outcome entirely.

THE FINAL SURPRISE: CANADA TAXES WHAT THE U.S. DOESN'T

For many Canadians and Americans crossing back north, this is the moment that feels the most unfair.

Paul and Marissa assumed that because the U.S. treated their home as a principal residence, Canada would follow the same logic. After all, it was the same house, the same owners, the same years of living there.

Canada did not agree.

TWO COUNTRIES, TWO COMPLETELY DIFFERENT PHILOSOPHIES

The U.S. and Canada approach housing gains from fundamentally different perspectives.

In the United States:

- Up to $250,000 of gain (single) or $500,000 (married) may be excluded on a principal residence, provided the property meets the IRS "2 out of 5 years" ownership and use test
- The exemption applies only for the portion of gain attributable to the qualifying period; if the home is sold after five years, the full exemption may not be availableMany long-term homeowners pay little or no federal tax on the sale

In Canada:

- The principal residence exemption applies only to Canadian property
- **Foreign properties may qualify for the PRE** if you were a Canadian resident and the property meets the PRE requirements under CRA rules
- **Gains on U.S. real estate are calculated using a stepped-up cost basis** equal to the fair market value on the date you became a Canadian resident, which can reduce the taxable gain

Paul put it simply:

"How can the same house be tax-free there and taxable here?"

The answer is uncomfortable but clear:

Canada taxes worldwide gains of its residents, without carving out foreign housing exemptions.

WHY THIS CATCHES PEOPLE OFF GUARD

Most people assume tax systems will "line up" through treaties.

The Canada–U.S. tax treaty:

- Prevents double taxation in many cases
- Allows foreign tax credits
- Does not force Canada to adopt U.S. housing exemptions

So even if:

- The U.S. owes nothing on the sale, and
- FIRPTA withholding is later refunded,

Canada may still assess a significant capital gains tax.

THE COMPOUNDING EFFECT

This mismatch often creates secondary consequences:

- Higher marginal tax rates in the year of sale
- OAS clawbacks for retirees
- Loss of income-tested benefits
- Surprise instalment requirements for future years

Because the U.S. doesn't warn sellers—and CRA doesn't either—many people discover this only after the fact.

WHAT COULD HAVE HELPED

Work with a cross-border tax accountant prior to selling. This is one area where a cross-border financial advisor cannot fully resolve the technical U.S. and Canadian tax issues.

THE REALITY

Neither country is "wrong."

They are simply operating under different rules.

But when a property crosses borders, the stricter system usually wins.

WHERE THIS LEAVES YOU

Cross-border real estate transactions involve multiple financial systems. Selling a U.S. property and purchasing a Canadian home requires awareness of tax reporting, withholding obligations, and currency considerations.

Because these factors interact across both countries, careful planning and professional guidance are essential to prevent unexpected costs or administrative complications.

In the concluding section, we'll pull these threads together and explain why real estate is often the most misunderstood—and most expensive—cross-border move of all, and how proper planning changes the outcome entirely.

CHAPTER 6
I HAVE U.S. INVESTMENTS — NOW WHAT?
TRANSITIONING PORTFOLIOS WHEN RETURNING TO CANADA

In This Chapter, You Will Learn...

In this chapter, you will learn why U.S. investments often become the most disruptive part of returning to Canada—and why problems usually begin only after you update your residency.

Specifically, this chapter explains:

- Why U.S. brokerage firms frequently freeze or restrict accounts once a Canadian address is added
- Why attempting to "just keep a U.S. address" creates serious compliance, tax, and account-closure risks
- How foreign mutual funds can trigger PFIC reporting requirements once Canadian residency resumes; U.S.-domiciled mutual funds generally do not trigger IRS PFIC rules
- Why the timing of selling, transferring, or restructuring
- U.S. investments can materially change your tax outcome
- Where U.S. dividend-paying stocks are most efficiently held after returning to Canada—and where they are not
- How Canadian residency changes the way you should think about CAD vs. USD exposure, cash flow, and long-term strategy
- Why employer plans such as 403(b)s, ESOPs, and deferred compensation become more complex across borders
- Why most advisors and platforms can only see one side of a cross-border financial life
- How a dual-licensed cross-border advisor restructures U.S. assets into a compliant, coordinated portfolio

- The most common and costly investment mistakes returning Canadians make—and how to avoid them

This chapter provides a practical framework for understanding what happens to U.S. investments when residency changes—and how to transition portfolios deliberately, rather than reacting after accounts freeze, penalties arise, or options disappear.

WHEN U.S. BROKERAGE ACCOUNTS FREEZE

For most returning Canadians, the first sign that something has gone wrong with their U.S. investments is a simple message:

"Account restricted."

This usually happens after updating their address to Canada.

U.S. brokerage firms are required to reassess whether they can legally continue servicing the account.

This is not based on performance or creditworthiness, but compliance with U.S. securities law.

Once Canadian residency is established, U.S. brokerage firms must comply with U.S. regulations:

- Trading privileges may be restricted or removed.
- New purchases may be blocked.
- Dividend reinvestment plans may be disabled.
- Accounts may be placed in "liquidation-only" status.

While the restrictions feel unfair, they're not personal. They're a regulatory response to residency changes, and they leave investors reacting instead of strategizing.

THE ADDRESS TRAP: WHY YOU CAN'T "JUST KEEP A U.S. ADDRESS"

After U.S. brokerage restrictions kick in, many returning Canadians receive the same well-meaning advice:

"Just keep a U.S. address. Everyone does it."

On the surface, it seems harmless. But in reality, it creates serious compliance risks.

Using a U.S. address after establishing Canadian residency is a compliance violation. Brokerage firms treat addresses as legal declarations of residency, and discrepancies in residency can result in:

- Regulatory risks for the firm.
- Inaccurate tax reporting: U.S. tax forms may be issued incorrectly, and Canadian reporting may become incomplete.
- Account freezes and forced liquidations.

Many investors think they can "fix it later," but once misrepresentation is suspected:

- Accounts are locked.
- Transfers are blocked.
- Liquidations are forced.

Once Canadian residency is confirmed, all accounts must reflect that reality. Relying on a U.S. address is only a temporary solution—and a risky one.

THE LIQUIDATION DILEMMA: WHY TIMING CAN MAKE OR BREAK YOU

When Canadians realize that their U.S. investments are no longer viable under Canadian residency, the question becomes unavoidable:

"Do I have to sell everything?"

The decision often depends on timing, not just the assets themselves.

- For investors who are U.S. persons (citizens or green card holders), selling too soon may trigger U.S. capital gains tax in addition to Canadian tax once residency is established.
- For non-U.S. persons, Canadian residency generally determines Canadian tax liability, and there may be no U.S. tax on liquidation.
- Selling too late can lead to forced liquidations or frozen accounts.

U.S.-domiciled mutual funds are not considered PFICs, so PFIC classification does not apply to these holdings.

The key to minimizing tax impact is timing:

- Before residency: The sale is generally subject only to U.S. tax treatment for U.S. persons.

After residency: Canadian taxes apply, calculated using a **stepped-up adjusted cost base** equal to the fair market value at the date Canadian residency begins. For non-U.S. persons, this can significantly reduce taxable gains.

SELLING TOO SOON: THE HIDDEN COST OF ACTING TOO FAST

Many investors liquidate U.S. investments prematurely due to fear or uncertainty, without fully understanding cross-border tax implications.

- **U.S. persons:** Selling too soon can trigger **unnecessary capital gains tax** for U.S. persons but upon establishing Canadian residency, the stepped-up adjusted cost base applies for Canadian tax purposes, so they are not exposed to taxation in both jurisdictions.
- Foreign tax credits may be available for U.S. tax paid, but **errors in claiming the credit correctly** can diminish its value.
- Income spikes from capital gains could push individuals into higher Canadian tax brackets, further increasing the total tax burden.
- **Non-U.S. persons:** When Canadian residency is established, both U.S. and non-U.S. persons benefit from a **stepped-up adjusted cost base,** reducing Canadian taxable gains. Selling after residency and after becoming a non-U.S. person **avoids U.S. taxation entirely**. Timing the sale strategically ensures that capital gains are taxed correctly and only in Canada.

The timing of the sale should be driven by strategic planning rather than fear. Understanding how residency changes affect taxes is key to making a well-timed decision.

SELLING TOO LATE: WHEN ACCOUNTS STOP COOPERATING

Waiting too long to sell U.S. investments after moving to Canada can trigger significant problems. Once Canadian residency is established, brokerage firms may:

- Restrict trading activity
- Prohibit new purchases
- Block reinvestment of dividends
- Freeze transfers
- Place accounts in "liquidation-only" status.

At that point, investors lose control over:

- Timing
- Pricing
- Strategic decisions

Moreover, holding certain securities for too long after residency changes can lead to:

- Inability to restructure holdings
- Ongoing compliance exposure
- Escalating accounting and reporting costs

This is when forced liquidation occurs—not on the investor's terms, but at a moment of regulatory control.

WHY RESIDENCY TIMING IS THE PIVOT POINT

The timing of Canadian residency, in addition to your your U.S. tax status, is the most critical factor in determining tax outcomes when selling U.S. assets.

- Before residency: Gains are generally taxed under U.S. tax rules for U.S. persons. For non-U.S. persons, gains are taxable in the U.S. only if they are considered U.S. resident aliens at the time; otherwise, non-U.S. persons are generally not subject to U.S. tax.
- After residency: Canadian tax laws apply, and U.S. persons continue to have U.S. reporting obligations. Non-U.S. persons are taxed in Canada on capital gains from their investment portfolio.

The key to minimizing tax impact is understanding exactly when Canadian residency starts:

- Timing the sale before residency can avoid Canadian tax.
- Timing the sale after residency requires careful allocation and reporting to mitigate tax exposure.

JOHN'S REALIZATION

John, a U.S. person, hadn't made any reckless decisions—he had simply waited, assuming he had time to strategize.

But time was already running out.

By the time he understood the full impact of his timing, his options were shrinking. Some sales needed to happen immediately, others needed to be delayed, and a few were better avoided entirely.

What became clear was this:

Liquidation is not just about deciding what to sell. It's about when to sell.

Handled properly, it can reduce taxes and preserve flexibility. Handled poorly, it locks in losses that are unrelated to market conditions.

WHERE U.S. DIVIDEND STOCKS BELONG AFTER RETURNING TO CANADA

Once John understood that selling everything was not always required, a more precise question emerged:

"If I keep my U.S. stocks, where should I hold them?"

This is one of the most misunderstood — and most expensive

decisions returning Canadians make.

The problem is not the stocks themselves. Companies like Apple, Microsoft, Procter & Gamble, or JPMorgan remain solid businesses regardless of where you live. The issue is account placement.

The same U.S. dividend-paying stock can be:

- tax-efficient in one account,
- tax-inefficient in another, and
- outright punitive in a third.

THE TREATY RULE MOST CANADIANS NEVER LEARN

Under the Canada–U.S. tax treaty, U.S. dividends held inside an RRSP or RRIF are exempt from U.S. withholding tax.

That means:

- No 15% U.S. withholding at source on dividends
- Full dividends received and reinvested
- Cleaner reporting on the Canadian side

Caution: If U.S. dividend shares are transferred from a non-registered U.S. cash account into an RRSP and the investor is a **U.S. person**, this can trigger a **deemed disposition** and potential U.S. capital gains.

For a **non-U.S. person resident in Canada**, any U.S. withholding can typically be claimed as a **foreign tax credit** on the Canadian return. In some cases, it may be more tax-efficient to **transfer the shares in-kind** to a Canadian RRSP

Advice: Speak with a **cross-border tax accountant** to ensure the most tax-efficient approach for your situation.

Many returning Canadians miss this opportunity simply because their accounts were not restructured in time.

WHY THE TFSA IS USUALLY THE WORST PLACE

A common mistake is placing U.S. dividend stocks inside a TFSA.

While the TFSA is tax-free in Canada, the U.S. does not recognize it as a registered account.

As a result:

- U.S. dividends are subject to 15% withholding tax
- That tax is non-refundable
- No foreign tax credit is available in Canada

Over time, this quietly erodes returns — especially for investors relying on dividend income.

HOLDING U.S. DIVIDEND STOCKS IN TAXABLE ACCOUNTS

Taxable (non-registered) accounts sit somewhere in between.

In these accounts:

- The U.S. withholds 15% at source
- Canada taxes the full dividend
- A foreign tax credit can be claimed for the U.S. tax withheld on the Canadian tax return which may partially offset the Canadian tax

This structure can work, but it requires:

- Proper T1135 reporting
- Careful tracking of foreign tax credits
- Awareness of how dividend income affects marginal tax rates and benefits such as OAS

Without coordination, what looks manageable on paper becomes messy in practice.

JOHN'S "AHA" MOMENT

John had spent years choosing *what* to invest in. He had never thought seriously about *where* those investments lived.

Once his advisor explained the difference, the strategy clicked:

"It's not about changing my stocks. It's about changing the containers."

By moving U.S. dividend stocks into treaty-protected accounts and reserving other structures for different asset types, John preserved income that would otherwise have leaked away through withholding and mismatched tax rules.

WHY THIS DECISION MUST COME BEFORE EXECUTION

Account placement decisions should be made before residency changes or forced account restrictions limit your options.

Once accounts freeze or transfers are blocked, the ability to optimize placement shrinks dramatically.

Understanding where U.S. dividend stocks belong is one of the simplest ways to improve after-tax outcomes — but only if the structure is put in place early enough.

In the next section, we'll explore how returning Canadians must rethink CAD versus USD exposure, and why currency becomes a strategy — not a transaction — once you're living back in Canada.

TAX-EFFICIENT CAD VS. USD ALLOCATION: A NEW WAY OF THINKING

After restructuring where his U.S. dividend stocks belonged, John assumed the hardest decisions were behind him. They weren't.

The next realization came quietly, but it changed how he viewed his entire portfolio:

Currency itself had become a planning issue.

While living in the United States, John's portfolio had naturally drifted toward U.S. dollars. His income, expenses, taxes, and investments all moved in the same currency. That alignment disappeared the moment he returned to Canada.

WHY CURRENCY STOPS BEING NEUTRAL AFTER YOU MOVE HOME

Once Canadian residency resumes, daily life is funded in Canadian dollars:

- housing
- groceries
- utilities
- insurance
- healthcare
- taxes

Yet many returning Canadians still hold the majority of their assets in USD.

That mismatch creates risk:

- currency swings affect lifestyle spending
- forced conversions occur at bad rates
- income timing becomes unpredictable
- tax bills arrive in CAD while assets sit in USD

Currency exposure is no longer just about returns — it directly affects cash flow stability.

THE COMMON OVERCORRECTION MISTAKE

Some returning Canadians react by converting everything to CAD immediately.

This can be just as damaging:

- large one-time FX losses
- poor timing during unfavorable exchange rates
- unnecessary capital gains
- loss of natural USD hedging for future U.S. expenses

The goal is not to eliminate USD exposure. The goal is to align currency with purpose.

A PRACTICAL FRAMEWORK FOR POST-RETURN ALLOCATION

For many returning Canadians, a more balanced approach emerges:

CAD holdings typically support:

- daily living expenses
- short-term liquidity
- Canadian taxes
- tax-efficient Canadian dividend paying stocks
- domestic investment needs

USD holdings often remain useful for:

- U.S. travel and lifestyle costs
- U.S. dividend income
- legacy U.S. assets

- diversification
- long-term growth exposure

This is not a one-size-fits-all model, but it highlights the shift in thinking required.

WHY TIMING AND TAX MUST BE COORDINATED

Currency moves are never just currency moves.

Converting USD to CAD can trigger:

- capital gains or losses
- changes in taxable income
- benefit clawbacks
- reporting obligations

When done without planning, currency decisions amplify tax problems instead of solving them.

John's advisor helped him stagger conversions, coordinate them with tax years, and preserve flexibility — turning currency into a tool rather than a liability.

FROM TRANSACTION TO STRATEGY

Before returning to Canada, John viewed currency as a simple exchange step.

After restructuring, he understood the difference:

- Transactions react to the moment.
- Strategies anticipate the future.

This shift allowed his portfolio to support his lifestyle instead of fighting it.

In the next section, we'll look at ESOPs and 403(b) plans, and why employer-based U.S. accounts often become the most difficult assets to untangle after a return to Canada.

WHY MOST ADVISORS CAN ONLY SEE HALF THE PICTURE

John's experience revealed a key problem: no one professional could see the full financial picture.

- U.S. financial advisors focused on SEC and FINRA rules, but couldn't offer insight into Canadian tax implications.
- Canadian and U.S. tax accountants were experts in CRA and IRS compliance but lacked experience with cross-border asset management.
- Canadian financial advisors handled Canadian investments but didn't coordinate tax strategies across borders.

Each advisor addressed only part of the issue, and their advice often conflicted. The lack of integrated guidance led to:

- Frozen accounts
- Duplicated reporting
- Unnecessary liquidations

THE STRUCTURAL BLIND SPOT IN CROSS - BORDER ADVICE

Most financial professionals are licensed, trained, and regulated within a single country.

That creates a built-in limitation:

- U.S. advisors are generally prohibited from advising Canadian residents
- Canadian advisors are restricted from advising on U.S.-domiciled accounts
- Accountants are typically trained in one tax system, not two
- Custodians enforce residency rules mechanically, without context

No one person is empowered — or permitted — to see the whole structure unless they are specifically licensed to do so.

John wasn't facing bad advice.

He was facing *partial advice.*

HOW FRAGMENTED GUIDANCE CREATES EXPENSIVE OUTCOMES

Each advisor addressed what they could see:

- His U.S. advisor focused on SEC and FINRA rules
- His Canadian advisor focused on CRA compliance
- His accountant focused on filing requirements
- His bank focused on custody and residency

Individually, each recommendation sounded reasonable.

Collectively, they conflicted.

The result was:

- frozen accounts
- duplicated reporting
- unnecessary liquidations
- missed treaty protections
- avoidable tax exposure

No one was coordinating the decisions — and no one was responsible for the full outcome.

WHY CROSS-BORDER PROBLEMS ESCALATE QUIETLY

Cross-border issues rarely explode immediately. They accumulate.

A frozen account today becomes a forced liquidation later. A missed filing this year becomes penalties three years from now.

An incorrect structure compounds across multiple tax cycles. By the time the damage is visible, it is often expensive to unwind. John summed it up simply:

"Everyone was helping — just not together."

WHAT A DUAL-LICENSED, CROSS-BORDER ADVISOR ACTUALLY DOES DIFFERENTLY

When John finally worked with a properly licensed cross-border advisor, the experience felt fundamentally different.

Instead of isolated fixes, the advisor:

- evaluated U.S. and Canadian residency simultaneously
- coordinated tax treatment under the treaty
- aligned account structures with custodial rules

- addressed reporting on both sides proactively
- sequenced actions to minimize friction and tax cost

Most importantly, decisions were made with awareness of both systems — not just one.

THE CORE LESSON OF THIS SECTION

The core lesson from this section is clear: Cross-border investing is complicated because the rules are divided between two countries.

- U.S. financial systems operate under U.S. law.
- Canadian systems operate under Canadian law.

Professionals trained in one system cannot fully understand or advise on the other. Without someone coordinating both systems, mistakes are almost inevitable, leading to:

- Conflicting advice
- Uncoordinated decisions
- Expensive mistakes

WHEN JOHN FINALLY SETTLED HIS PORTFOLIO

By the time John reached this stage, the damage had not come from bad investing. It came from misalignment.

Nothing about his portfolio was reckless. He held well-known companies, diversified funds, and employer plans that had served him well for decades. The problem was that his financial structure was still designed for a life in the United States, while he was now living in Canada.

Once John engaged a properly cross-border team, the work was not about chasing returns. It was about restoring order.

The first step was platform alignment. His assets were transferred to a dual-licensed, cross-border compliant platform that was permitted to service Canadian residents without triggering account freezes or forced liquidations. This single change removed the constant risk of sudden restrictions.

Dividend-paying U.S. stocks were repositioned into treaty-protected structures where possible. Holding location—not ownership—became the focus. Once John understood that the same investment could be efficient or inefficient depending on where it sat, his decisions became clearer.

Employer plans followed. His 403(b) was rolled into an IRA where appropriate. ESOP reporting was corrected. IRS and CRA filings were coordinated so that income was recognized once, not twice, and reported consistently across both systems.

Currency was addressed last, not first. Rather than reacting to exchange rates, a longer-term CAD and USD strategy was built around cash-flow needs, future U.S. travel, and tax timing. Currency conversion stopped being a transaction and became part of an overall plan.

John summed it up simply:

"I didn't know how complicated my financial life had become until someone finally laid it out in one place."

What changed was not just the structure of his portfolio, but his confidence. For the first time since returning to Canada, he understood where his investments belonged, why they were held that way, and how both tax systems interacted.

This was not optimization. It was stabilization.

CONCLUSION — RETURNING CANADIANS NEED A PATH, NOT PATCHWORK

Crossing the border does not simply change where you live—it transforms how your investments are taxed, structured, and reported.

John's experience highlights the costly mistakes many Canadians make when their financial lives are split between two systems without coordination.

The solution is not just to optimize U.S. investments but to reframe them.

- Where assets are held is just as important as what those assets are.

- Timing and structure matter—decisions made in isolation can lead to irreparable financial damage.

For returning Canadians, the key is planning, not improvisation.

A coordinated strategy ensures that U.S. investments remain productive, compliant, and seamlessly integrated into Canadian life.

CHAPTER 7
HEALTHCARE SHOCK: LEAVING U.S. COVERAGE & REQUALIFYING FOR PROVINCIAL HEALTH PLANS

INTRODUCTION — "WAIT... WE'RE NOT COVERED?"

For Susan and Mark, returning to Canada after more than twenty years in the United States felt like a homecoming in every sense of the word. They had planned carefully. Their finances were organized. Their taxes were addressed. Their move across the border went smoothly.

Healthcare, they assumed, would be the simplest part of the transition.

After all, they were Canadian citizens. They had lived in British Columbia before. Canada had universal healthcare. The idea that they could be uninsured—even briefly—never crossed their minds.

Three days after arriving, Susan called to confirm their enrollment in British Columbia's Medical Services Plan (MSP). She expected a routine confirmation.

Instead, the agent calmly explained that their coverage would begin on the first day of the third month after arrival.

Susan paused, certain she had misunderstood. "You mean... we're uninsured for three months?"

"Yes," the agent replied. "There is a waiting period."

In that moment, Susan realized something that almost every returning Canadian eventually learns—often the hard way:

Coming home to Canada does not mean coming home to healthcare coverage immediately.

The following ninety days would become one of the most stressful periods of Susan and Mark's relocation. Not because of illness, but because of uncertainty. They were healthy, careful, and financially responsible—yet completely exposed.

This chapter exists because that exposure is not rare. It is normal.

Healthcare is one of the most misunderstood aspects of cross-border moves. People assume continuity where none exists. They assume citizenship equals coverage. They assume past residence guarantees immediate access. They assume U.S. insurance will "bridge the gap."

None of those assumptions hold once you cross the border.

Healthcare does not switch on and off like a light. It transitions—and that transition is often rough, expensive, and emotionally jarring if you are unprepared.

PROVINCIAL WAIT PERIODS — THE FIRST SHOCK

The first healthcare surprise most returning Canadians encounter is the provincial waiting period.

Canada's healthcare system is universal, but it is administered at the provincial level. Each province sets its own rules for reinstating coverage when someone returns after living abroad. The result is a patchwork of timelines, documentation requirements, and interpretations of "residency."

For Susan and Mark, the shock came quickly.

In British Columbia, Medical Services Plan (MSP) coverage begins on the first day of the third month after arrival. The rule is rigid. If you arrive on March 10, coverage does not begin until June 1. There are no exceptions for long-time citizens, former residents, or retirees.

Other provinces apply similar—but not identical—rules:

- Ontario (OHIP):
  Coverage begins **immediately upon establishing residency**, as the previous three-month waiting period was eliminated in March 2020.

Proof of residency and intent to remain may still be required for certain administrative purposes.

- Alberta (AHCIP):
  Coverage can begin immediately, but only if the returning resident can prove an intention to remain in Alberta for at least twelve months. This often requires employment documentation, housing arrangements, or other formal ties.
- Saskatchewan and Manitoba:
  Coverage is often immediate, but strong documentation is required, and interpretation can vary.
- Quebec (RAMQ):
  Reinstatement frequently involves delays and requires clear proof of settlement and residency.
- Atlantic provinces:
  Tend to be more flexible, but still require evidence that the return is permanent rather than temporary.

What surprises most people is not the existence of these rules—it is how inflexible they can be. Provincial health plans do not operate on sentiment or past contribution. They operate on administrative definitions of residency and timing.

Susan and Mark learned what thousands before them have discovered:

Canadian healthcare is universal—but it is not instant.

That gap between arrival and coverage is where the real risk lives. And for most returning Canadians, that gap is wider than they ever imagined.

THE INSURANCE GAP — AND THE FIRST BILL

The second shock arrives quickly—and usually with paperwork attached.

Susan assumed that her U.S. employer-sponsored health insurance would protect them during the transition period. After all, she had paid into the plan for years. The move back to Canada was recent. MSP hadn't started yet. Surely there was some overlap.

There wasn't.

The moment Susan left her job, her employer plan ended. There was no grace period tied to geography, and no exception for international relocation. Employer-sponsored health insurance in the United States is exactly that—employment-based. Once employment ends, so does coverage.

Susan then assumed COBRA would step in as a safety net. It didn't.

COBRA continuation coverage applies only under very specific conditions. It is designed for individuals who remain U.S. residents and continue to receive care within the United States. Once Susan updated her address to British Columbia, the assumptions underlying COBRA no longer applied. Residency matters. Location of care matters. Crossing the border changed both.

Travel insurance also failed them—something Susan wouldn't fully understand until later.

So when Mark slipped while unloading boxes during their first week home and fractured a rib, the consequences were immediate and tangible.

At the Vancouver emergency room, there was no discussion of coverage. There was no automatic billing to MSP. There was no "we'll sort it out later."

The bill was issued directly to them.

$1,200 — due immediately.

Mark stared at the invoice, confused. "I thought healthcare was free." Susan understood now.

"It is," she said quietly. "But not yet."

This moment captures the essence of the insurance gap that returning Canadians face. It is not theoretical. It is not rare. It is the predictable result of systems that do not overlap or coordinate.

On one side of the border, U.S. coverage ends cleanly and decisively. On the other side, Canadian coverage begins only after administrative conditions are met. In between, there is often nothing.

This gap is where financial risk turns into emotional stress. People are careful. They delay appointments. They second-guess symptoms. They worry not just about health, but about cost.

What makes this gap particularly dangerous is that most people do not know it exists until they are standing inside it—injured, uninsured, and surprised.

In the next section, we will look at one of the most common assumptions people make to try to bridge this gap—and why it fails almost every time.

WHAT HAPPENS TO MEDICARE?

Mark had done what he was supposed to do.

When he turned 65 in the United States, he enrolled in Medicare Part A and Part B on time. No delays. No penalties. No gaps. His coverage worked exactly as advertised while he lived in Colorado.

So when they returned to Canada, Mark assumed Medicare would operate the same way travel insurance had in the past—dormant but usable if needed.

It wasn't.

Medicare does not travel with you.

The moment Mark crossed into Canada, Medicare became effectively inactive—not cancelled, not terminated, but unusable outside the United States. It would not pay for:

- Doctor visits
- Diagnostic tests
- Specialists
- Hospital stays
- Emergency care

In practical terms, Medicare became a card that only worked if Mark physically returned to the U.S. for care.

This creates a counterintuitive problem for returning Canadians who are Medicare-eligible:

you may need to keep paying for coverage you cannot use, just to avoid future penalties.

WHY DROPPING PART B IS SO DANGEROUS

Many people assume the logical move is to cancel Medicare Part B once they leave the U.S. That decision often comes back to haunt them.

If Mark were to drop Part B and later decide to return to the U.S.—even part-time—he would face:

- Lifetime late-enrollment penalties
- A higher Part B premium forever
- Delayed re-enrollment windows
- Potential coverage gaps upon return

These penalties accumulate at roughly 10% for every 12 months you were eligible but not enrolled. Over time, that becomes expensive—and permanent.

This is why many cross-border advisors recommend maintaining Medicare enrollment even while living in Canada, despite the frustration of paying premiums for coverage that cannot be used locally.

It feels irrational. It is, unfortunately, rational under U.S. rules. What Medicare is — and is not — after you leave

For returning Canadians, Medicare becomes:

- A future access credential for U.S. care
- A risk-management tool if you return south
- A cost you carry during your Canadian transition

It is not:

- A bridge to Canadian healthcare
- A substitute for provincial coverage
- A solution for the insurance gap

Mark described it bluntly:

"We were paying for something we couldn't use, because not paying would punish us later."

That trade-off—pay now to avoid permanent penalties later—is one of the least understood aspects of cross-border healthcare planning.

And it reinforces a central theme of this chapter: healthcare systems do not coordinate with each other. They protect themselves first.

In the next section, we look at another assumption that fails the moment you cross the border—U.S. private insurance, employer plans, and COBRA—and why they stop the instant residency changes.

WHAT ABOUT U.S. PRIVATE HEALTH INSURANCE?

After the Medicare shock, Susan turned to what had always worked in the past: employer-sponsored private insurance.

Her plan had been excellent.

Broad coverage. Predictable copays. Familiar providers.

For years, it had been the backbone of their healthcare security in the U.S.

So she did what many returning Canadians do—she assumed she could simply extend it temporarily while Canadian coverage caught up.

That assumption failed immediately. Why employer plans stop at the border

U.S. private health insurance is territorial. It is built to function inside the U.S. healthcare system, under U.S. regulation, with U.S. providers.

Once Susan left her job and updated her address to British Columbia:

- Her employer coverage ended
- Out-of-country claims were denied
- Reimbursements stopped processing
- The plan was no longer valid

Even though she was still paying premiums.

From the insurer's perspective, nothing had gone wrong. The contract was simply no longer applicable. Coverage was tied to:

- U.S. employment

- U.S. residency
- U.S.-based care

Change any one of those, and the policy collapses.

WHY COBRA DOESN'T SOLVE THE PROBLEM

Susan's next idea was COBRA. After all, COBRA is marketed as a safety net—temporary continuation of employer coverage after leaving a job.

But COBRA has strict boundaries:

- It applies only to U.S. residents
- It requires a U.S. address
- It covers care delivered in the United States
- It assumes the policyholder remains within the U.S. healthcare system

Once Susan formally relocated to Canada:

- Claims for Canadian care were rejected
- Address verification flagged the account
- Coverage was terminated

COBRA did exactly what it was designed to do. It just wasn't designed for cross-border transitions.

THE CORE MISUNDERSTANDING

Most returning Canadians believe one of the following:

- "I'll keep my U.S. plan until provincial coverage starts"
- "I'll use COBRA as a bridge"
- "I'll submit claims later"
- "It worked when we traveled—why not now?"

The difference is intent and residency.

Travel insurance and employer plans are structured for temporary absence, not relocation. The moment you "take up residence" in Canada—even if provincial coverage hasn't started—you are no longer viewed as a covered U.S. resident temporarily abroad.

Your status changes. Your coverage ends.

Susan's advisor explained it plainly:

"U.S. insurance doesn't follow you. It protects people who live there."

THE EMOTIONAL COST OF THIS REALIZATION

This was the point where Susan felt truly exposed. They had:

- No U.S. coverage
- No Canadian coverage
- No private Canadian option yet
- No employer benefits
- No reimbursement path

They were healthy. But health is unpredictable.

And the next section would make that painfully clear—because even when people think they've protected themselves with travel insurance, that protection disappears the moment a move becomes a relocation.

In the next section, we look at why travel insurance stops working the moment you 'move home', and why that misunderstanding causes some of the most expensive mistakes returning Canadians make.

COORDINATING MEDICAL RECORDS — A NIGHTMARE

Susan's Colorado cardiologist was confident the transition would be simple.

"Your new doctor can just pull your records."

It sounded reasonable. After all, healthcare is digital now. Everything lives in electronic systems. Surely doctors can share information across borders.

They can't.

WHY MEDICAL RECORDS DON'T MOVE WITH YOU

U.S. and Canadian healthcare systems operate on entirely separate infrastructures:

- Different electronic medical record (EMR) platforms
- Different privacy laws and consent standards

- No shared databases
- No automatic cross-border access

Canadian clinics cannot "pull" records from U.S. hospitals. Even within Canada, record transfers are often manual. Across borders, they become the patient's responsibility.

Susan learned this the hard way.

THE ADMINISTRATIVE BURDEN NO ONE WARNS YOU ABOUT

To rebuild her medical history in British Columbia, Susan had to:

- Contact multiple U.S. providers individually
- Complete authorization forms for each office
- Pay record retrieval and processing fees
- Track down specialists she hadn't seen in years
- Explain medications by U.S. brand names unfamiliar to Canadian physicians
- Print records that didn't integrate with Canadian systems

Each step required time, follow-up, and persistence—exactly when she was already overwhelmed by relocation stress.

WHEN "DIGITAL" TURNS OUT NOT TO BE MODERN

The breaking point came when her Colorado clinic mailed her diagnostic imaging... on a CD-ROM.

Her new BC doctor stared at it and said:

"We haven't used disc drives in years."

The files were useless without conversion. Reports had to be reissued. Tests were duplicated. Appointments were delayed.

Susan sat in her car afterward and cried.

Healthcare was supposed to be easier in Canada. Instead, it felt fragmented, outdated, and inaccessible—because the system had no memory of her past.

WHY THIS MATTERS MORE THAN INCONVENIENCE

This isn't just frustrating. It's risky. Incomplete medical histories can lead to:

- Delayed diagnoses
- Medication errors
- Repeated testing
- Missed allergies or prior complications
- Conservative treatment decisions based on missing data

Canadian physicians rely heavily on documented history. Without it, they often start from zero.

THE PATTERN MOST RETURNEES EXPERIENCE

Almost every returning Canadian discovers the same thing:

- Doctors assume records will follow
- Records don't
- Patients become the courier
- Important details get lost
- Care slows down at the worst possible moment

This is why experienced cross-border advisors recommend preparing medical records before the move, not after.

Susan didn't know that. Most people don't.

In the next section, the shock shifts from administration to affordability—because once coverage and records are sorted out, returning Canadians discover something else that changes overnight: the cost of medications.

PRIVATE CANADIAN INSURANCE — NOT WHAT MOST THINK

After the shock of prescription costs, Susan did what most returning Canadians instinctively do.

"I'll just buy private insurance until MSP starts."

It sounded reasonable. It felt responsible.

It was almost impossible.

THE ASSUMPTION THAT DOESN'T HOLD

Most Canadians grow up believing private insurance can always step in when public coverage isn't active. That belief comes from how extended health benefits work after provincial enrollment.

But private Canadian insurers do not operate as primary healthcare providers.

They are designed to *supplement* provincial plans—not replace them.

Susan learned this the hard way. The answer every insurer gave She contacted multiple providers:

- Manulife
- Sun Life
- Blue Cross
- GMS
- Several regional insurers

Each conversation ended the same way:

"We cannot insure you until you have provincial healthcare coverage."

The reasoning was simple but unforgiving:

- Provincial plans are expected to cover core medical services
- Private insurers only layer benefits on top
- Without MSP, OHIP, or equivalent coverage, the risk profile is too high

No provincial coverage meant no private Canadian coverage.

WHAT PRIVATE PLANS ACTUALLY COVER

Once provincial healthcare is active, private plans typically cover:

- Prescription drugs (partially)
- Dental and vision
- Physiotherapy and massage
- Mental health services

- Medical equipment

What they *do not* cover as standalone insurance:

- Hospital stays
- Emergency room visits
- Diagnostic imaging
- Specialist consultations

These are assumed to be provided by the province.

During the waiting period, those assumptions collapse.

THE LIMITED OPTIONS THAT REMAIN

With Canadian private insurance unavailable, Susan and Mark were left with only a handful of imperfect options:

International expat plans

Often expensive, medically underwritten, and restrictive.

Coverage may exclude pre-existing conditions or limit Canadian-based care.

Newcomer transition plans

Designed primarily for immigrants—not returning citizens—and frequently capped at low limits.

Canadian employer benefits

Only available if one spouse is actively employed and eligible immediately.

A U.S. Health Savings Account (HSA)

The one tool that continued to function seamlessly across borders.

Note: Investments held in U.S. HSA accounts are **taxable for Canadian tax purposes**, even though the account retains its U.S. HSA status.

Each option came with trade-offs. None resembled the comprehensive coverage they expected.

WHY THIS GAP IS SO DANGEROUS

This is the period when risk is highest:

- People are exhausted from moving
- Medical records are in transit
- Doctors are unfamiliar
- Stress levels are elevated
- Coverage assumptions are wrong

One emergency during this window can undo years of careful financial planning.

Susan described it bluntly:

"We felt like we were uninsured in a country famous for healthcare."

THE STRUCTURAL MISUNDERSTANDING

The problem isn't that Canada lacks healthcare. The problem is timing and structure.

Canadian healthcare assumes:

- Long-term residency
- Continuous enrollment
- Provincial administration
- Employer-based supplements

Cross-border moves break all four assumptions at once.

That's why so many returning Canadians are caught off guard—and why healthcare planning must be treated as a transition process, not an automatic entitlement.

In the next section, Susan discovers the one healthcare tool that *does* cross the border cleanly—and becomes unexpectedly indispensable during the most vulnerable phase of their return.

WHEN EVERYTHING FINALLY SETTLED

By the time Susan and Mark's MSP coverage finally activated, nearly three months had passed since they crossed the border. Those ninety days had reshaped how they thought aboutmhealthcare—not as a given, but as a system that must be actively rebuilt.

Relief came first. Then clarity.

With provincial coverage in place, their cross-border advisor helped them step back and stabilize what had felt like constant triage:

- Medicare was preserved correctly, avoiding future penalties while accepting that it would remain dormant unless they returned to the U.S.
- The HSA was repositioned as a long-term supplemental healthcare reserve rather than an emergency-only account.
- Medical records were consolidated, translated into Canadian-compatible summaries, and properly archived for future specialists.
- Prescriptions were re-evaluated, switching to Canadian equivalents where possible and budgeting for medications that remained expensive.
- Employer benefits were coordinated, ensuring no overlap gaps or double premiums.
- Healthcare costs during the waiting period were documented, allowing them to understand exactly what the transition had cost—and how to prevent it in the future.

What surprised Susan most wasn't the complexity—it was how predictable the process became once someone explained the sequence.

"The stress wasn't because the system was broken," she said later.

"It was because we didn't know the order things were supposed to happen in."

Once the timeline made sense, healthcare stopped feeling like an emergency and started feeling manageable again.

They hadn't just regained coverage.

They had rebuilt a healthcare strategy that actually fit their new life in Canada.

CONCLUSION — HEALTHCARE IS A TRANSITION, NOT A SWITCH

Most returning Canadians believe one simple thing:

"I'll have healthcare the day I arrive."

Chapter 17 exists to gently—but firmly—correct that assumption.

The moment you cross the border:

- U.S. employer coverage ends
- Travel insurance voids
- COBRA stops applying
- Medicare becomes inactive in Canada
- Private Canadian insurers won't step in
- Provincial healthcare imposes waiting periods
- Medical records don't transfer cleanly
- Prescription costs change—sometimes dramatically

Healthcare does not flip on and off like a light switch.

It transitions.

And that transition requires:

- Understanding provincial timelines
- Planning for uncovered months
- Knowing which tools still work (and which don't)
- Budgeting realistically
- Coordinating records, medications, and benefits
- Avoiding assumptions that no longer apply

Susan and Mark didn't do anything reckless.

They did what thousands of returning Canadians do—assume the system would recognize them automatically.

It didn't.

This chapter exists so others don't learn these lessons:

- In an emergency room

- With a surprise bill
- While injured, sick, or scared
- Wondering why "universal healthcare" suddenly feels
- unfamiliar

With preparation, healthcare can be one of the most reassuring parts of returning home.

Without it, it becomes one of the most painful.

Healthcare isn't something you regain by arriving.

It's something you rebuild—step by step—once you do.

CHAPTER 8
IMMIGRATION REALITIES WHEN MOVING BACK TO CANADA
WHAT RETURNING CANADIANS AND U.S. FAMILIES MOVING NORTH MUST UNDERSTAND

INTRODUCTION — "HOW DID WE END UP HERE?"

Moving back to Canada isn't as simple as packing boxes and crossing the border. Many families assume that their citizenship, marriage, or good intentions will make the process automatic.

However, immigration is more than paperwork. It involves intent, timing, and documentation. These elements shape your tax obligations, healthcare access, and benefits.

This chapter is for those who need to understand the real-world immigration issues that appear during cross-border moves, including the misunderstandings that often arise when people assume the process is easier than it is.

IMMIGRATION BASICS FOR RETURNING CANADIANS

Even Canadian citizens must follow specific immigration procedures when returning after living abroad.

While Canadian citizenship allows entry without a visa, re-establishing active residency involves more than just crossing the border.

Returning Canadians must prove:

- Intent to reside in Canada permanently.
- Provincial residency for healthcare and benefits.
- Proof of settlement (e.g., Canadian lease, utility accounts, Canadian bank activity).

Canada doesn't automatically recognize you as a resident simply because you are a citizen. The immigration system requires proof of your intent to live and settle, affecting your access to various services.

FOR AMERICANS MOVING TO CANADA

Unlike returning Canadians, Americans don't have the automatic right to live in Canada.

Moving north requires specific immigration pathways, even for those who feel connected to the country.

Common misconceptions include:

- Dual tax residency: Many Americans mistakenly assume that because they have ties to Canada, their tax status will automatically align with their immigration status. However, U.S. tax obligations continue until proper immigration status is obtained.
- Physical presence rules: Canadians may need to meet minimum physical presence requirements, which is often confusing for those who've lived close to the border or frequently visit.

Americans moving to Canada need a clear immigration plan that aligns with the Canadian immigration system, not assumptions based on familiarity.

FOR CROSS-BORDER COUPLES

Marriage doesn't automatically resolve immigration status for cross-border couples. While being married to a Canadian may make you eligible for sponsorship, it doesn't guarantee immediate residency.

Key considerations include:

- Sponsorship delays: Even married couples face months of waiting for sponsorship approval, often up to a year or more.
- Work permits: Spouses may not be authorized to work during the sponsorship process.
- Healthcare access: Provincial healthcare eligibility may be delayed until the residency status is finalized.

- Proof of relationship: Documentation, including shared finances, a lease, or evidence of cohabitation, may be required.

While marriage creates eligibility for sponsorship, immigration approval involves a detailed process that can take time and careful planning.

FOR FAMILIES WITH CHILDREN

When moving to Canada with children, families face unique challenges that go beyond just immigration. Key considerations include:

- School enrollment requirements: Many provinces require proof of Canadian residency and immigration status before children can be enrolled in public schools.
- Healthcare access: Provincial healthcare often requires a waiting period, so families may need private insurance during the transition period.
- Citizenship vs. residency: It's important to understand that citizenship alone doesn't guarantee full access to all services. Residency status must be re-established, and this affects healthcare, schooling, and other services.

Understanding these requirements early ensures a smoother transition for children and avoids delays or confusion with schooling and healthcare access.

FOR WORKERS MOVING NORTH

When relocating to Canada for work, it's essential to understand how employment offers must align with Canadian immigration requirements. Simply having a job offer is not enough—specific conditions must be met:

- Employment offers must meet IRCC requirements: The offer must be detailed and meet the standards set by Immigration, Refugees and Citizenship Canada (IRCC).
- Work permits: Many workers require a work permit, even if they already have a job offer. It's crucial to apply for the correct type of permit before entering Canada.

- Remote work complications: U.S. remote workers may assume that working from Canada for a U.S. employer won't require Canadian immigration documentation. This is not the case—working in Canada without the proper status can lead to legal and tax issues.

Without proper coordination between immigration status and work permits, workers can face delays, penalties, or even inability to work in Canada.

FOR RETIREES

Retirees face some of the longest delays in immigration processing due to specific documentation requirements and verification of intent to reside. Canada does not offer an automatic retirement visa, so retirees must meet the same immigration requirements as other residents.

Key considerations include:

- Proving intent to live in Canada permanently: Retirees must demonstrate that they are actively establishing residency in a specific province.
- Healthcare eligibility: Provinces often impose waiting periods, and proof of residency is required before retirees can access healthcare.
- Retirement income: Retirees may need to provide evidence of sufficient financial resources to support themselves without relying on Canadian social services.

These requirements make retirement planning more complex than many retirees expect, but with the right guidance, the process can be manageable.

WHY IMMIGRATION MUST BE COORDINATED WITH TAX PLANNING, INVESTMENT STRUCTURE, AND HEALTHCARE TIMING

Immigration to Canada isn't just about crossing the border—it's a multifaceted process that affects tax residency, investment strategies, and healthcare access. Immigration timing directly impacts all of these areas, so planning needs to be coordinated.

Key points to consider:

- Tax implications: The timing of your immigration determines whether you're taxed in the U.S., Canada, or both. Early or delayed immigration decisions can lead to dual taxation or missed tax relief opportunities.
- Investment structure: U.S. investments like mutual funds and retirement accounts can be subject to complex rules when brought into Canada. Without proper planning, you may face unwanted tax penalties.
- Healthcare eligibility: Some provinces impose a waiting period for healthcare coverage, which can leave you vulnerable if you're not covered by private insurance during the transition.

Without careful coordination, your financial and healthcare situation can become fragmented, leading to costly mistakes.

"THE PODCAST CALL WE NEVER EXPECTED"

Two weeks after returning from Maui, another productive recording trip filled with interviews, listener questions, and cross-border case discussions, I opened my inbox and saw a message I won't forget.

"Gerry, we listened to your podcast. Can you help us move home?"

Attached was a photo of a couple standing in front of their Scottsdale home, smiling, but with the kind of tension you can see even in a still image. They had lived in the U.S. for 31 years.

Three children. Four jobs. A lifetime of memories.

And now they wanted to come home to Canada, but had no idea how immigration, taxes, healthcare, and financial systems would collide the moment they crossed the border.

That same week, five more messages arrived:

- A Canadian nurse returning from California
- A couple retiring from Austin after 20 years
- An American man moving to Vancouver to marry his Canadian fiancée

- A family from Florida seeking Permanent Residency
- A dual-citizen teenager unsure whether he must "sponsor himself"

This is why we do the podcast.

This is why cross-border education matters.

Because the pattern is consistent. People are not careless. They are simply operating on ideas they have heard for years: that citizenship solves everything, that marriage grants instant approval, that you can enter as a visitor while you "figure things out," that benefits restart automatically when you come home.

Then they collide with the real system.

And in immigration, the collision often happens at the border, with consequences that are hard to undo once the wrong step is taken.

"I'M CANADIAN, SO I'M AUTOMATICALLY BACK IN THE SYSTEM... RIGHT?"

This is the moment where most returning Canadians feel blindsided—not because they did something wrong, but because they assumed the system would recognize them automatically.

"I'm Canadian," they say.

"I was born here."

"I paid taxes here before."

"I've come home."

What they discover instead is this:

Canada welcomes you back as a citizen, but it treats your return as a new arrival event, not a continuation of your past life.

Citizenship and residency are not the same thing.

WHY CITIZENSHIP DOESN'T EQUAL "ACTIVE RESIDENCY"

From an immigration perspective, Canadian citizens do not need permission to enter the country. There is no visa to apply for and no approval letter to wait on. That part is true.

But everything that follows—healthcare, taxes, benefits, banking access, provincial services—depends not on citizenship, but on re-established residency.

When you return after living abroad for years or decades, Canada expects you to actively prove that you are living in the country again. Until you do, many systems remain paused or inaccessible.

This is where expectations and reality diverge.

WHAT RETURNING CANADIANS ARE REQUIRED TO DO

Upon return, Canadians are expected to re-establish themselves administratively, often from scratch. This typically includes:

- Re-establishing provincial residency
- Re-registering for healthcare
- Updating or reactivating a Social Insurance Number record
- Providing proof of permanent settlement
- Demonstrating intent to live full-time in a specific province
- Triggering Canadian tax residency
- Registering or re-registering for provincial programs and services

None of this happens automatically at the airport.

From the government's perspective, living abroad severed your active ties. Returning means rebuilding them—and the burden of proof sits with you.

THE ROLE OF " INTENT TO RESIDE"

One of the most misunderstood concepts in Canadian systems is intent.

Intent to reside is not a feeling. It is not nostalgia. It is not citizenship. It is demonstrated through actions and documentation.

Examples of what provinces and agencies often look for include:

- A Canadian lease or home purchase
- Utility accounts in your name
- Canadian banking activity
- Provincial driver's license or ID
- Employment or business ties

- School enrollment for children
- Evidence that U.S. ties have been reduced or severed

Without these signals, returning Canadians are often treated cautiously—not as visitors, but not fully as residents either.

This affects far more than immigration status.

WHY THIS MISUNDERSTANDING CAUSES DOWNSTREAM PROBLEMS

When people assume they are "automatically back in the system," they often act too quickly or in the wrong order.

They may:

- Apply for healthcare before they can prove residency
- Trigger tax residency earlier than expected
- Close U.S. accounts before Canadian systems are ready
- Assume benefits will restart immediately
- Move dependents without understanding provincial requirements

Each of these missteps creates friction—not because the system is hostile, but because it operates on rules that do not match common assumptions.

The system does not ask, "Are you Canadian?"

It asks, "Are you living here now, and can you prove it?"

THE EMOTIONAL DISCONNECT

Moving to Canada isn't just a financial and legal process—it's also an emotional transition. Many returning Canadians experience a disconnect between their expectations and the realities of settling back home.

The emotional challenges include:

- Uncertainty about the future: Many returning Canadians are unsure about how they'll adapt to a system they haven't experienced in years.
- Loss of community: The transition means leaving behind social networks, friends, and work relationships.

- The burden of choice: With two systems to navigate, many feel overwhelmed by the sheer number of decisions that need to be made.

Understanding these emotional challenges and preparing for them is just as important as planning the logistics of the move. Managing expectations and addressing these concerns can help ease the transition.

THE KEY TAKEAWAY

The core message of this chapter is clear: immigration to Canada isn't just about moving—it's about properly coordinating multiple systems.

Immigration timing affects tax obligations, investment strategies, and healthcare access, all of which must be planned in advance.

Key takeaways:

- Early planning is essential for avoiding tax residency issues and ensuring seamless access to healthcare.
- Coordination between tax planning, investment structure, and immigration status ensures a smoother transition.
- Ignoring timing or documentation requirements can lead to unnecessary complications, delays, and financial costs.

"I THOUGHT WE COULD JUST MOVE TO CANADA."

This is one of the most common—and most costly—assumptions Americans make when heading north.

They fall in love with Canada first. The cities.

The pace.

The safety.

The lifestyle.

Then they assume the move itself will be straightforward. It isn't.

WHY AMERICANS CANNOT " JUST MOVE" TO CANADA

Unlike returning Canadians, Americans have no automatic right to live in Canada, regardless of how long they have visited, how close they live to the border, or how familiar they feel with the country.

For Americans, entry and long-term stay in Canada must fit into specific immigration categories recognized by Immigration, Refugees and Citizenship Canada (IRCC).

These include:

- Family sponsorship
- Skilled worker pathways
- Intercompany transfers
- Study permits
- Provincial Nominee Programs
- Start-up visas
- Temporary foreign worker permits

If you do not qualify under one of these frameworks, you do not have legal status to live in Canada—no matter how sincere your intentions are.

Driving across the border with moving boxes does not create residency.

Renting a condo does not create residency.

Planning to "figure it out later" does not create residency.

THE VISITOR STATUS TRAP

One of the most damaging mistakes Americans make is entering Canada as a visitor while intending to move permanently.

From the traveler's perspective, it feels harmless: "We'll go up, get settled, and apply once we're there."

From CBSA's perspective, it can be misrepresentation. Visitor status is granted on the assumption that:

- You are entering temporarily
- You do not intend to reside permanently

- You will leave at the end of your authorized stay

When someone enters as a visitor but behaves like a resident—bringing household goods, enrolling children in school, starting work, or giving up U.S. ties—it creates a contradiction that border officers are trained to identify.

And when they do, the consequences can be immediate.

WHAT MISREPRESENTATION LOOKS LIKE IN PRACTICE

CBSA officers are not looking for trickery. They are looking for intent.

Red flags often include:

- A vehicle full of personal belongings
- Canadian lease agreements
- School enrollment letters
- Job offer documents without proper permits
- Pets being transported permanently
- Statements like "we're moving" instead of "we're visiting"

When intent and status don't align, entry can be denied—even if no laws were knowingly broken.

This is how families end up:

- Turned around at the border
- Issued removal orders
- Flagged for future entry
- Delayed by months or years

And once misrepresentation is recorded, fixing it becomes far more complicated.

WHY AMERICANS UNDERESTIMATE CANADIAN IMMIGRATION

Many Americans subconsciously compare Canada to another U.S. state.

The cultures feel familiar.

The language is the same.

The border feels friendly.

But immigration law does not care about familiarity.

Canada's system is points-based, category-driven, and documentation-heavy. It is designed to filter eligibility—not accommodate lifestyle preferences.

Unlike some countries, Canada does not offer:

- A general retirement visa
- A "self-funded resident" option
- Automatic pathways for long-term visitors

This is particularly shocking for retirees and remote workers, who often assume financial independence alone will qualify them.

It doesn't.

WHERE AMERICANS GO WRONG EMOTIONALLY

Most Americans don't ignore the rules—they misunderstand them.

They assume:

- Marriage will fix everything
- Remote work is automatically allowed
- Crossing first and applying later is acceptable
- Good intentions matter more than process

Immigration systems don't operate on intent alone. They operate on structure.

And that structure must be respected before the move, not retroactively.

THE KEY TAKEAWAY

For Americans, immigration status is not a formality—it is the foundation.

Every other system depends on it:

- Tax residency
- Healthcare eligibility
- Employment legality
- Banking access
- School enrollment

- Long-term planning

If immigration is mishandled at the start, everything built on top of it becomes unstable.

In the next section, we bring both sides together—Canadians and Americans alike—and examine the most common cross-border immigration mistakes that derail otherwise well-planned moves.

COMMON CROSS-BORDER IMMIGRATION MISTAKES WHERE OTHERWISE SENSIBLE PLANS GO OFF THE RAILS

By the time families reach out for help, the problem is rarely that they ignored immigration rules entirely.

It's that they relied on assumptions that *felt* logical—but don't hold up inside Canada's immigration framework.

Across hundreds of cases, the same mistakes appear again and again.

MISTAKE #1 — ASSUMING MARRIAGE EQUALS AUTOMATIC APPROVAL

This is one of the most persistent myths.

Marrying a Canadian does not grant immediate residency, work authorization, or healthcare access.

In reality:

- Sponsorship applications take months, sometimes more than a year
- Background checks, medical exams, and financial reviews are mandatory
- The sponsored spouse may not be allowed to work during parts of the process
- Provincial healthcare often remains unavailable until status is finalized

Couples are often shocked to learn that being legally married does not equal being legally resident.

Marriage creates *eligibility to apply*—not automatic status.

MISTAKE #2 — "WE'LL MOVE FIRST AND HANDLE THE PAPERWORK LATER"

This approach works in almost no immigration system, and Canada is no exception.

Canada expects:

- Proof of eligibility before benefits are granted
- Proof of intent to reside before healthcare enrollment
- Proof of status before work, school, or long-term residence

When families move first, they often find themselves in limbo:

- Living in Canada but not legally resident
- Paying Canadian costs without Canadian benefits
- Unable to work, enroll children, or access services

What feels like a head start becomes a delay.

MISTAKE #3 — USING THE WRONG STATUS FOR REMOTE WORK

Remote work has created enormous confusion.

Many Americans assume:

"I'm working for a U.S. employer, so Canada doesn't care."

Canada *does* care.

Depending on the situation:

- Remote work may still be considered work performed in Canada
- Visitor status may prohibit any form of employment
- The wrong permit can invalidate status entirely

This is one of the fastest ways to trigger border scrutiny, future entry issues, or compliance problems that bleed into tax and payroll obligations.

MISTAKE #4 — NOT COORDINATING IMMIGRATION WITH TAX RESIDENCY

Immigration residency and tax residency often start on different days.

A person may:

- Become a Canadian tax resident before immigration status is finalized
- Trigger worldwide taxation without healthcare access
- Create reporting obligations before benefits begin

When these timelines aren't aligned, families face:

- Double taxation risks
- Missed filings
- Incorrect assumptions about coverage and entitlements

Immigration is not isolated. It sets the clock for everything else.

MISTAKE #5 — IGNORING HEALTHCARE WAITING PERIODS

Immigration approval does not equal healthcare coverage. Even with proper status:

- Provinces impose waiting periods
- Proof of settlement is still required
- Coverage gaps remain common

Families assume immigration success means protection. It doesn't.

THE PATTERN BEHIND THESE MISTAKES

None of these errors come from recklessness.

They come from applying *domestic logic* to an international system.

People assume:

- Good faith will be enough
- Systems will coordinate
- Someone will "tell them" if something is wrong

Immigration systems don't work that way.

They respond to documentation, timing, and status—not intention.

In the next section, we step back and explain why immigration decisions quietly shape every other part of a cross-border move, even when families don't realize it yet.

WHY IMMIGRATION & FINANCIAL PLANNING ARE ONE AND THE SAME

The Hidden Chain Reaction Most Families Miss

Most families treat immigration as a standalone task: "Once we're approved, we'll deal with everything else."

In reality, immigration is the first domino. Once it falls, everything downstream changes.

THE SEQUENCE MOST PEOPLE DON'T SEE

Many people think of immigration as a single event—a straightforward move from one country to another. However, the process is more like a domino effect. Each decision you make about your immigration status triggers a sequence of financial, tax, and healthcare implications.

Key points in the sequence:

- Immigration timing affects tax residency, which in turn affects capital gains tax and foreign asset reporting.
- Health coverage eligibility begins with provincial residency, which starts the clock on waiting periods.
- Tax strategies must align with both U.S. and Canadian regulations to avoid dual taxation and ensure proper credit claims.

Ignoring the sequence can result in mismatched actions, leading to unnecessary tax penalties, delayed healthcare, and missed opportunities.

HOW IMMIGRATION TIMING AFFECTS TAXES

The timing of your immigration to Canada directly impacts your tax residency status, which determines how you're taxed on global income.

Key points:

- Before immigration: If you sell assets or earn income,
- U.S. tax laws apply.

- After immigration: Once Canadian tax residency is established, Canadian tax laws come into effect, including taxation on global income.
- Dual taxation: Timing mistakes, such as entering Canada too early or too late, can lead to being taxed under both U.S. and Canadian laws, requiring careful coordination.

Understanding and planning the timing of your residency can help avoid dual taxation and ensure you minimize tax exposure across both countries.

HOW IMMIGRATION STATUS AFFECTS INVESTMENTS

When moving to Canada, your immigration status directly impacts your investment strategy. U.S. investments, such as mutual funds, stocks, and retirement accounts, are subject to different tax rules depending on your residency.

Key points:

- Retirement accounts: U.S. 401(k)s and Traditional IRAs are generally tax-deferred under the Canada–U.S. treaty. Income accrues tax-free in Canada and is taxed only upon distribution.
- Capital gains: The sale of U.S. assets after moving to Canada may result in Canadian capital gains tax on investments that were previously subject to U.S. tax.

Proper planning ensures that investments are structured in a way that minimizes tax liabilities in both countries.

HOW HEALTHCARE DEPENDS ON IMMIGRATION PROOF

Provincial health plans require:

- Proof of legal right to reside
- Proof of intent to remain
- Proof of physical presence

Immigration delays often mean:

- Extended uninsured periods

- Rejected applications
- Requests for additional documentation

Healthcare does not activate on goodwill. It activates on status. Why advisors must work together

This is why experienced cross-border planning requires coordination between:

- Immigration attorneys
- Tax professionals
- Investment advisors
- Healthcare and benefits specialists

When these professionals work in isolation, families become the messenger—and critical details are lost.

When they work together, timelines align.

THE CORE LESSON

The core lesson is simple: Planning is everything. Cross-border moves require careful coordination between immigration status, tax obligations, investment strategies, and healthcare access. Ignoring any of these aspects can lead to unnecessary complications, financial penalties, and lost opportunities.

Key points:

- Timing your immigration properly is crucial for tax planning.
- Immigration decisions affect your investment structure and healthcare eligibility.
- Coordination is essential to ensure all these systems work together smoothly, minimizing risks and maximizing benefits.

HOW IMMIGRATION MISSTEPS SHOW UP IN REAL LIFE

Many returnees face unexpected challenges when their immigration plans don't align with tax, financial, and healthcare systems. Missteps often occur due to:

- Uncoordinated immigration timing: Moving without understanding the full impact on tax residency and healthcare access.
- Failure to document intent to reside: This can delay healthcare coverage and tax status.
- Incorrect assumptions about benefits: Many expect immediate access to Canadian benefits and services without meeting the provincial residency requirements.

These issues become evident once practical steps—like tax filings or healthcare registration—are needed, and can result in:

- Unnecessary penalties
- Delayed services
- Missed opportunities for tax relief

THE RETURNING CANADIAN TOLD TO "PROVE SHE ACTUALLY LIVES HERE"

A Canadian citizen returned to British Columbia after twenty-eight years in Texas. She expected her MSP application to be routine.

It wasn't.

The province requested proof that she was truly resident—not visiting, not transitioning, not undecided.

She was asked to provide:

- Utility bills
- A lease agreement
- Canadian banking activity
- Evidence that U.S. ties had been severed

Until she did, her healthcare application stalled.

Citizenship brought her home. Residency had to be proven.

THE AMERICAN RETIREE WITH NO ELIGIBLE PATHWAY

Another listener planned to retire to Canada after years of vacationing there.

He had:

- No Canadian spouse
- No Canadian employer
- No business sponsorship
- No provincial nomination

What he discovered—too late—was simple and shocking: Canada does not have a retirement visa.

Without a qualifying category, there was no legal pathway for him to settle permanently, no matter how peaceful his intentions or how long he had dreamed of it.

WHAT THESE STORIES HAVE IN COMMON

Each case reflects a different life situation, but they share a single theme:

Immigration decisions are based on status, not sympathy.

Canada is welcoming—but structured. It does not infer intent. It requires proof.

These stories are why education matters. Not to scare families—but to prevent them from learning these lessons at the border, with children in the back seat or boxes packed at home.

In the next section, we zoom out and explain why immigration outcomes quietly shape *everything else*—from taxes to healthcare to financial planning—even when families don't realize it yet.

IMMIGRATION SHAPES EVERYTHING ELSE

WHY NOTHING IN A CROSS-BORDER MOVE IS TRULY SEPARATE

Families often think of immigration as a single hurdle to clear.

In reality, it is the frame that holds the entire cross-border move together.

IMMIGRATION DETERMINES TIMING

Before anything else can happen, immigration status answers foundational questions:

- When does residency legally begin?
- When can you work?
- When can children attend school?
- When do healthcare clocks start?
- When do tax obligations activate?

Without clear status, every other system hesitates.

IMMIGRATION CONTROLS ELIGIBILITY

Almost every benefit returning Canadians or new arrivals expect is gated by immigration proof:

- Provincial healthcare
- Child benefits
- Tuition classification
- Employment authorization
- Access to regulated financial advice

Even Canadian citizens returning after decades abroad must demonstrate current residency—not historical connection.

IMMIGRATION AFFECTS TAX RESIDENCY—BUT NOT ALWAYS ON THE SAME DAY

One of the most dangerous misconceptions is assuming immigration status and tax residency begin simultaneously.

They often don't.

It's entirely possible to:

- Become a Canadian tax resident before immigration status feels "settled"
- Trigger worldwide taxation before healthcare begins
- Create filing obligations before benefits activate

This mismatch is why immigration must be coordinated with tax planning—not handled in isolation.

Immigration impacts financial structure

Banks, brokerages, and advisors rely on immigration facts to determine:

- Which accounts can remain open
- Which investments are permitted
- Which advisors are legally allowed to advise you
- Whether accounts are frozen, restricted, or closed

Families often interpret these changes as financial problems. They are immigration-triggered compliance responses.

Why professional coordination matters

This is why experienced cross-border planning always involves collaboration:

- Immigration attorneys who understand status and pathways
- Tax professionals who understand residency triggers
- Financial advisors licensed to work across borders
- Healthcare planners who understand provincial rules

When these professionals work independently, families absorb the friction.

When they work together, transitions become predictable.

Organizations like Immigration, Refugees and Citizenship Canada set the legal framework—but families live with the practical consequences.

The core lesson

Immigration is not just about permission to enter or stay. It sets:

- The timeline for benefits
- The start of tax obligations
- The availability of healthcare
- The structure of finances
- The stability of family life

Handled early and correctly, it becomes invisible.

Handled late—or assumed—it becomes the source of nearly every downstream shock.

In the final section of this chapter, we return to reflection—why this work matters, and why immigration is not just law, but the beginning of someone's next chapter.

CONCLUSION — "THE MOST GRATEFUL PART OF MY CAREER"

When I look back over my journey—from my first trip to the United States in 1981, to beginning my career in financial services in 1994, and helping cross-border families over the past decade—one feeling outweighs everything else: gratitude.

Gratitude for the families who trust us with moments that matter deeply:

- Deciding where to raise children
- Choosing where to retire
- Reuniting families across borders
- Starting over in a familiar country that has quietly changed

And gratitude for the immigration professionals—particularly the attorneys in both Canada and the United States—who patiently help us navigate a system that has grown more complex, more regulated, and more unforgiving over time.

Immigration is not a side issue

What this chapter has tried to make clear is something many families only realize after the fact:

Immigration is not paperwork you complete after you decide to move.

It is the structure that determines whether your move actually works.

It defines:

- When you are allowed to be present
- When you are allowed to work
- When your children can attend school
- When healthcare begins
- When tax obligations activate
- When financial accounts change treatment

Every other system—tax, investment, healthcare, benefits—takes its cues from immigration status and timing.

Why so many families are caught off guard

Most people do not misunderstand immigration because they are careless.

- They misunderstand it because:
- They assume citizenship equals residency
- They assume marriage equals approval
- They assume intent is obvious
- They assume systems communicate with each other
- They assume moving "home" is different from immigrating

In practice, immigration systems do not operate on assumption. They operate on documentation, categories, and dates.

Canada is welcoming—but procedural.

The United States is familiar—but territorial.

Neither system adapts itself to personal history unless the law explicitly allows it.

The privilege of being part of the beginning

What makes this work meaningful is not the forms, the rules, or the regulations.

It's the moments behind them:

- A family crossing the border with certainty instead of fear
- A couple reunited without unnecessary delay
- Parents enrolling children in school without last-minute panic
- Retirees settling in with clarity instead of constant compliance anxiety

Immigration is not just law.

It is the beginning of someone's next chapter.

And being trusted to help families begin that chapter—properly, legally, and with their eyes open—is something I never take for granted.

This chapter exists so fewer families have to say:

"We thought moving to Canada would be simple."

And more families can say:

"We knew what to expect—and we planned for it."

That difference changes everything.

CHAPTER 9
FINANCES, BANKING & CREDIT BUILDING A LIFE IN CANADA — EVEN WHEN YOUR CREDIT HISTORY IS AMERICAN

For many returning Canadians and Americans moving north, credit history is a significant concern. In Canada, your U.S. credit score does not transfer, which can make securing loans, mortgages, or even renting property more difficult.

Key challenges include:

- No direct transfer of U.S. credit: Canadian financial institutions do not access U.S. credit reports, so a strong
- U.S. history won't automatically build Canadian credit.
- Building Canadian credit: You'll need to establish credit in Canada from scratch, either by getting a Canadian credit card or securing a small loan to start your Canadian credit profile.
- Credit history overlap: While Canadian lenders may consider your U.S. credit history, they will generally require Canadian-based financial activity to assess your creditworthiness.

By starting early and managing Canadian credit responsibly, you can build your financial reputation in Canada, making it easier to transition to everyday life without financial setbacks.

CREDIT SCORES DON'T CROSS THE BORDER — NOT EVEN A LITTLE

Your U.S. credit score does not transfer to Canada, leaving many newcomers to start from scratch when building their credit profile in Canada.

Key challenges:

- No automatic transfer: Canadian financial institutions do not access U.S. credit reports, so your credit history in the U.S. has no bearing on your Canadian creditworthiness.
- Building Canadian credit: You'll need to establish a credit history by applying for a Canadian credit card or loan to start building your Canadian credit profile.

Despite having a solid U.S. credit history, you'll need to prove your financial reliability within Canada to access credit, loans, or mortgages.

CREDIT INVISIBILITY VS. POOR CREDIT

Credit invisibility occurs when you don't have a Canadian credit history, even if you've had good credit in the U.S.

The challenge isn't that you have poor credit—it's that no Canadian credit report exists for you to build upon. This makes it harder to access credit in Canada.

Key points:

- Credit invisibility: Without a credit history in Canada, you're essentially "invisible" to Canadian lenders, even if your U.S. credit history is excellent.
- Poor credit: If you have poor credit, Canadian lenders can see your bad history and may be hesitant to approve you for loans or credit.
- Both situations require you to start building a Canadian credit history from scratch.

WHY U.S. LENDERS DON'T HELP

U.S. lenders typically do not support Canadian residents in building or maintaining Canadian credit. This happens because:

- Different credit systems: The U.S. operates on a different credit system, and Canadian credit history is not automatically linked to U.S. credit reports.

- Regulatory restrictions: U.S. lenders are not obligated to share Canadian credit information with U.S. credit bureaus, creating a gap in credit reporting.
- Cross-border complexities: Even though you may have a good credit score in the U.S., Canadian banks are unfamiliar with it and do not integrate it into their own credit assessment.

Because of these limitations, U.S. lenders cannot help you build Canadian credit or assist with Canadian-specific financial products.

THE EMOTIONAL IMPACT NO ONE WARNS YOU ABOUT

Moving to Canada is not just a financial or logistical challenge—it's also an emotional journey. Many newcomers experience frustration, uncertainty, and loss of community as they navigate the complexities of starting fresh in a new country.

Common emotional challenges include:

- The feeling of starting over: After building a life in the U.S., it can feel overwhelming to face the bureaucracy and financial systems of Canada from scratch.
- Loss of connections: Moving away from friends, family, and familiar networks can create feelings of isolation and homesickness.
- Distrust and infantilization: Many newcomers feel disrespected or treated as financial novices, even after years of managing their finances in the U.S.

Understanding these emotional hurdles and managing expectations can help ease the transition and make the process feel less daunting.

THE KEY MINDSET SHIFT

The key to navigating the cross-border move is adopting the right mindset. Instead of focusing on what's lost, focus on what can be built. Transitioning from the U.S. to Canada requires a shift in perspective:

- Embrace change: The process is not about replicating your life in the U.S.; it's about building a new foundation in Canada.

- Be patient: Progress will take time—understanding that credit, banking, and even emotional connections will evolve gradually.
- Take control: Recognize that while systems are different, you are the one who drives the transition. Taking proactive steps will help you navigate the challenges.

This mindset shift allows newcomers to approach their financial and personal transition with confidence and clarity, rather than overwhelm.

THE FIRST FINANCIAL STEPS EVERY AMERICAN MUST TAKE

When moving to Canada, the first financial steps are crucial for establishing a stable foundation. Here's how to start:

Open Canadian bank accounts: Set up a Canadian checking account and savings account to integrate into the local financial system.

- Apply for a Canadian credit card: Start building Canadian credit early by applying for a secured credit card if needed.
- Establish proof of Canadian residency: Provide documentation, such as a lease agreement, utility bills, or Canadian bank statements, to prove your intent to settle.
- Ensure cross-border banking connections: Consider using international banks or services like American Express Global Transfer to maintain U.S. connections while you establish Canadian credit.

These first steps will set you up for financial success in Canada, allowing you to build credit history, manage expenses, and navigate Canadian financial products.

STEP 1: OPEN A CANADIAN CHEQUING ACCOUNT — THE ANCHOR POINT

Everything starts here.

Before credit, before investments, before payroll, you need a Canadian bank account. Not a USD account in Canada. Not a cross-border account. A domestic Canadian chequing account.

Banks will typically require:

- Passport
- Work permit, PR card, or proof of legal status
- Proof of Canadian address (lease, utility bill, or employer letter)
- SIN (if already issued — not always mandatory on day one)

This account becomes your financial anchor:

- Payroll deposits flow here
- Bills are paid from here
- Credit applications reference it
- CRA and provincial agencies link to it

Without it, nothing else moves.

STEP 2: APPLY FOR A CANADIAN CREDIT CARD — CAREFULLY

This is where most newcomers stumble.

Emily assumed she could walk in and apply for a standard credit card. That assumption would have triggered an immediate decline—and that decline would have stayed on her Canadian credit file, even before it was fully formed.

Instead, her advisor explained the correct hierarchy of options:

- Newcomer credit programs offered by major banks
- Secured credit cards if necessary
- American Express Global Transfer (when available)

The goal at this stage is approval, not prestige. A low-limit card that reports monthly is infinitely more valuable than a premium card you can't get.

STEP 3: GENERATE A CANADIAN CREDIT SCORE — PATIENCE REQUIRED

Canadian credit bureaus typically need at least 90 days of activity before generating an initial score.

During this phase, Emily followed strict rules:

- Kept utilization under 20%
- Paid balances weekly—not monthly
- Avoided cash advances entirely

- Never missed a payment, even by one day

This wasn't about maximizing rewards. It was about signaling

reliability to a system that knew nothing about her yet.

After three months, she had something she didn't before:

A visible Canadian credit profile.

STEP 4: ESTABLISH A CANADIAN PHONE PLAN

This step surprises many Americans.

In Canada, phone carriers are often stricter than banks. A postpaid phone plan is a form of credit. Without a credit file, newcomers are frequently asked for:

- Large deposits
- Prepaid plans
- Co-signers

Emily secured a modest postpaid plan early. That account:

- Reported to credit bureaus
- Added depth to her file
- Reinforced payment consistency

It wasn't glamorous—but it worked.

STEP 5: LOCK IN PAYROLL AND TAX RESIDENCY

Once payroll was established and taxes were being withheld in

Canada, Emily's financial identity officially flipped.

At this point:

- Canadian income was verifiable
- CRA recognized her as a resident taxpayer
- Lenders saw recurring domestic income
- Her profile began to "normalize" in underwriting
- systems

This step is critical. Without Canadian-source income, many lenders simply won't engage—no matter how strong your background is.

THE COMMON MISTAKE TO AVOID

The biggest error newcomers make is trying to skip steps:

- Applying for loans before building credit
- Requesting high limits too early
- Submitting multiple applications in frustration
- Assuming income alone solves everything Each decline slows the process.

Emily avoided that trap by treating her first six months not as a limitation—but as a setup phase.

As she later said:

"Getting hired was the easy part. Building a life here was the challenge."

In the next section, we'll look at the secret advantage that dramatically speeds this process for some newcomers: cross-border banking relationships—and why knowing which institutions talk to each other can save months of frustration.

CROSS-BORDER BANKING — THE SECRET ADVANTAGE

Cross-border banking offers a significant advantage when transitioning from the U.S. to Canada. Using banks that operate in both countries can help maintain financial continuity and streamline the integration process.

Key benefits include:

- Simplified money transfers: U.S. and Canadian accounts under the same bank make it easier to transfer funds between both countries without high fees.
- Consistent financial history: Certain banks recognize your U.S. credit history and help bridge the gap as you establish your Canadian credit.

- Convenience: Access to U.S. services in Canada, such as checking accounts, loans, and credit cards, without starting completely from scratch.

Banks like HSBC and Citi offer cross-border services, providing seamless connections for customers living between both countries.

THE BANKS THAT ACTUALLY OFFER CROSS-BORDER LEVERAGE

Emily's advisor walked her through the institutions that consistently offer workable cross-border onboarding:

- TD ↔ TD Bank USA
- Strong retail presence on both sides, especially for day-to-day banking and newcomers.
- RBC ↔ City National Bank (U.S.)
- Particularly useful for professionals, executives, and higher-net-worth clients.
- BMO ↔ BMO Harris
- Effective for credit cards, mortgages, and small business transitions.
- CIBC ↔ CIBC U.S.
- Helpful for basic banking and account continuity.
- Scotiabank ↔ global partners

Less U.S.-centric, but useful for international structures.

Each pairing has different internal programs. The advantage doesn't come from walking into a branch—it comes from being routed through the right onboarding channel.

AMERICAN EXPRESS GLOBAL TRANSFER — THE REAL SHORTCUT

For those transitioning between the U.S. and Canada, American Express Global Transfer offers a simple solution for maintaining credit continuity across borders.

Key benefits:

- Seamless credit transfer: American Express allows you to move your U.S. credit history to your Canadian account, making it easier to access credit in both countries.
- No credit score reset: Unlike opening a new credit card in Canada, this service ensures that your U.S. credit history is recognized, giving you a head start in building Canadian credit.
- Convenience: You can transfer points, maintain your U.S. account, and use the same American Express card in both countries.

By using American Express Global Transfer, you streamline your move, avoiding the gap that many people face when building Canadian credit from scratch.

WHAT CROSS-BORDER BANKING DOES—AND DOES NOT—SOLVE

Cross-border banking offers distinct advantages but does not solve everything for newcomers to Canada.

What it does solve:

- Simplified transfers: Moving funds between U.S. and Canadian accounts without excessive fees.
- Access to both countries' services: Enables seamless use of U.S. and Canadian financial products.
- Building credit history: Some institutions recognize
- U.S. credit and help bridge the gap when starting in Canada.

What it does not solve:

- Automatic credit history transfer: U.S. credit does not instantly integrate into Canadian systems, so newcomers still need to build Canadian credit from scratch.
- Health coverage or taxation: Cross-border banking doesn't affect eligibility for Canadian healthcare or solve dual taxation issues.

While cross-border banking offers clear advantages, it's not a one-stop solution for all financial needs when moving between countries.

WHY MOST NEWCOMERS MISS THIS ADVANTAGE

Many newcomers to Canada fail to take full advantage of cross-border banking because they overlook its potential benefits early in the process.

Common reasons:

- Lack of awareness: Newcomers may not realize that U.S. credit history can be recognized by Canadian banks, which gives them a head start in building Canadian credit.
- Not opening cross-border accounts early: Waiting too long to establish cross-border banking relationships can result in missed opportunities to bridge the gap between
- U.S. and Canadian financial systems.
- Assuming it's too complex: Many assume cross-border banking is complicated or doesn't apply to their situation, but it's an effective tool for maintaining financial continuity.

By actively seeking cross-border banking solutions, newcomers can more smoothly navigate their financial transition and avoid unnecessary delays in credit and banking integration.

THE HIDDEN PROBLEM: U.S. ACCOUNTS THAT FREEZE

When you move to Canada, U.S. accounts often freeze, creating an unexpected challenge. This happens because U.S. financial institutions must comply with regulations that require them to reassess your residency status when your address changes to Canada.

What happens:

- Automatic freezes: U.S. banks flag Canadian addresses and may restrict account activity or close accounts entirely.
- Tax compliance concerns: Address changes raise questions about U.S. tax residency, prompting account suspensions to comply with U.S. laws.

- Limited access: Your ability to access or transfer funds from U.S. accounts may be restricted.

To avoid this, notify your U.S. bank in advance about your move and maintain clear cross-border banking connections to keep your financial operations uninterrupted.

WHY U.S. BANKS FREEZE ACCOUNTS WHEN RESIDENCY CHANGES

Most Americans don't realize this, but U.S. banks are not allowed to freely service non-U.S. residents unless they hold specific cross-border licensing and compliance frameworks.

Once Emily updated her address to Canada, the bank was legally required to reassess:

- Whether it could continue servicing her
- Whether her account violated residency-based regulations
- Whether her activity triggered enhanced compliance scrutiny

From the bank's perspective, this wasn't punitive. It was procedural.

From Emily's perspective, it was terrifying.

WHAT " RESTRICTED" ACTUALLY MEANS

When U.S. banks flag a residency change, accounts are rarely closed immediately. Instead, they are often placed into one of several restricted states:

- Debit cards disabled
- Credit card transactions flagged or declined
- Online access limited
- New transfers blocked
- "Liquidation only" status for investment accounts
- Forced closure timelines quietly initiated

The worst part?

Many clients don't realize what's happening until they try to use the account—and can't.

BROKERAGE ACCOUNTS ARE EVEN MORE VULNERABLE

For Emily, the real shock came when she logged into her U.S. brokerage account.

A notice appeared:

"Due to a change in residency, your account functionality has been restricted."

This is extremely common with firms like:

- Schwab
- Vanguard
- Fidelity
- Merrill
- TD Ameritrade
- E*TRADE

These firms are regulated under U.S. securities laws that strictly limit servicing non-resident clients. Once residency changes, they may:

- Prohibit new trades
- Block reinvestment of dividends
- Prevent purchases of certain securities
- Force liquidation over time None of this is personal.

All of it is legal compliance.

THE MISTAKE THAT ACCELERATES FREEZES

Emily made the same mistake many newcomers make.

She updated *everything* at once:

- Address
- Phone number
- Country of residence
- Billing information

From a compliance standpoint, this was a red flag cascade.

To the bank's systems, it looked like:

- A foreign resident
- Accessing U.S. financial infrastructure
- Without a compliant servicing framework

The system responded exactly as designed.

WHY THIS PROBLEM CATCHES PEOPLE OFF GUARD

In the U.S., banks rarely explain residency-based servicing rules upfront. Clients assume accounts are permanent, portable, and universal.

They aren't.

Financial accounts are territorial.

They exist inside regulatory borders, not personal ones. Emily said later:

"I thought I was being responsible by updating my address. I didn't realize I was locking myself out."

HOW A DUAL-LICENSED ADVISOR PREVENTS THIS

This is where cross-border planning becomes critical.

A dual-licensed cross-border advisor:

- Knows which institutions can legally maintain accounts for Canadian residents
- Coordinates address changes strategically, not reactively
- Transfers assets before restrictions trigger
- Preserves U.S. credit history without misrepresentation
- Prevents account shutdowns that take years to reverse

Emily's advisor moved quickly.

Before more restrictions appeared:

- Certain accounts were transferred to compliant platforms
- Others were restructured or closed on Emily's terms
- Her remaining U.S. credit lines were stabilized legally

What felt like a financial emergency became a controlled transition.

THE LESSON MOST PEOPLE LEARN TOO LATE

This section exists for one reason:

Most Americans discover U.S. account freezes after they've lost access—when solutions are limited, expensive, and stressful.

Emily was lucky. She caught it early.

In the next section, we'll look at the moment that truly rattled her confidence—when one small administrative change caused her U.S. credit cards to be cancelled outright, and her hard-earned credit score to drop almost overnight.

WHY DID MY U.S. CREDIT CARD GET CANCELLED?

Emily thought she was fixing a small administrative detail.

She wasn't.

She was triggering one of the fastest—and most painful—financial consequences Americans experience after moving to Canada.

THE INNOCENT CHANGE THAT CAUSED REAL DAMAGE

Like most responsible people, Emily believed accuracy mattered. She logged into her U.S. credit card account and updated her billing address to match her new Canadian apartment in Victoria.

No warning appeared.

No confirmation message raised concern. No explanation followed.

Two days later, both of her U.S. credit cards stopped working.

At first, she assumed it was another temporary fraud alert. She called customer service expecting a quick fix.

Instead, she heard words that felt disproportionate to the

change she'd made:

"Your accounts have been closed due to a change in residency."

WHY U.S. CREDIT CARDS ARE BRUTALLY SENSITIVE TO RESIDENCY

Most major U.S. credit cards are issued under agreements that require:

- A U.S. residential address
- U.S. residency
- A U.S.-based billing profile
- Compliance with U.S. consumer lending regulations

When Emily changed her address, the issuer's system automatically reclassified her as a non-resident account holder.

That reclassification triggered mandatory actions:

- Immediate account review
- Suspension of charging privileges
- Closure of accounts that no longer met eligibility requirements

This wasn't a customer service decision.

It was a regulatory one.

WHY THE OLDEST CARDS ARE USUALLY THE FIRST TO GO

What shocked Emily most was which cards were closed.

Not the newer one.

Not the card she barely used.

Her oldest account—the one she'd had since college—was shut down first.

From a lender's perspective, older cards carry:

- Higher credit limits
- More historical exposure
- Greater regulatory scrutiny

From a credit-score perspective, losing that card was devastating.

THE HIDDEN CREDIT SCORE IMPACT

Within weeks, Emily's U.S. credit score dropped by nearly 80

points.

Not because she missed a payment. Not because she carried a balance. Not because she was reckless.

But because:

- Her average account age collapsed
- Her available credit shrank overnight
- Her utilization ratio spiked automatically

Emily had spent ten years building elite credit. It took one address update to dismantle it.

She said later:

"I didn't realize my credit history was tied to geography."

THE MISTAKE MOST AMERICANS MAKE

This scenario happens so often it follows a pattern:

- American moves to Canada
- Updates U.S. credit card address to be "honest"
- Issuer flags non-residency
- Cards are closed
- Credit score drops
- Reopening becomes nearly impossible

Once closed, these accounts are rarely reinstated—even if you later return to the U.S.

WHY KEEPING A U.S. ADDRESS IMPROPERLY IS NOT THE SOLUTION

Some people hear this story and think:

"I'll just keep a U.S. address."

That approach is dangerous.

Using a U.S. address when you no longer reside there can trigger:

- Account termination for misrepresentation
- Compliance investigations

- Permanent bans from certain issuers
- Issues if audited or reviewed later

There is a legal way to preserve U.S. credit.

And there is a risky way.

Only one works long-term.

HOW EMILY'S ADVISOR STABILIZED THE DAMAGE

Emily's dual-licensed cross-border advisor acted quickly. They:

- Identified which U.S. cards could be retained legally
- Shifted spending behavior to protect remaining credit
- Preserved reporting accuracy without misrepresentation
- Coordinated Canadian credit-building simultaneously
- Used Canadian-issued alternatives where appropriate

Most importantly, they reframed the strategy.

The goal was no longer "keeping everything the same."

It was transitioning without burning bridges.

THE EMOTIONAL TOLL OF CREDIT LOSS

Emily described this moment as the first time she truly felt financially vulnerable.

"It wasn't the money.

It was losing something I worked years to build—and not

knowing I was even at risk."

This section exists to make one thing clear:

U.S. credit cards do not fail gradually.

They fail decisively—often without warning—when residency changes.

In the next section, we'll explore another invisible cost of cross-border moves: currency conversion, and how banks quietly extract thousands from newcomers who don't know what to look for.

THE CURRENCY TRAP — HOW BANKS TAKE THOUSANDS WITHOUT ASKING

When moving between the U.S. and Canada, currency conversion is a hidden cost that many don't anticipate. Banks charge hidden spreads and fees when converting funds, significantly eroding wealth over time.

Key issues:

- Conversion fees: Banks often apply an unfavorable exchange rate, resulting in higher conversion costs than advertised.
- Hidden spreads: Even if a bank claims to offer a competitive rate, spreads between the buy and sell rates can lead to additional costs.
- Frequent small losses: With frequent transactions, even small discrepancies in exchange rates can add up to thousands in extra costs.

To minimize losses, it's essential to shop around for the best exchange rates and consider using specialized cross-border financial services that offer better rates than traditional banks.

THE TRANSFER THAT LOOKED HARMLESS

Shortly after settling in Victoria, Emily transferred $50,000 USD from her U.S. bank to her new Canadian account.

She didn't shop around.

She didn't ask questions.

She trusted the bank.

The transfer went through smoothly.

No warning screens appeared.

No fees were highlighted.

No red flags were raised.

Only later—when she compared exchange rates—did she realize something was wrong.

She hadn't lost money in the market. She had lost it in the spread.

HOW BANKS REALLY MAKE MONEY ON CURRENCY

Most people believe currency conversion fees look like this:

- "Fee: $X"

They don't.

Banks typically earn on foreign exchange through:

- Hidden exchange-rate markups
- Wide bid–ask spreads
- Non-transparent conversion rates
- Forced conversions at settlement

In Emily's case, the bank applied a spread of just over 3%. On a $50,000 transfer, that meant:

$1,500 disappeared instantly.

No invoice.

No receipt.

No clear disclosure.

Just less money arriving than expected.

WHY NEWCOMERS ARE ESPECIALLY VULNERABLE

Banks know something most newcomers don't yet understand:

Cross-border movers are:

- Time-constrained
- Overloaded with decisions
- Focused on logistics, not optimization
- Unaware that better options exist
- Likely to move large sums quickly

That makes them ideal candidates for high-margin FX transactions.

Emily said later:

"I didn't know moving countries meant donating money to the bank."

WHY "DOING IT ONCE" STILL MATTERS

Many people dismiss this loss by saying:

"It's a one-time thing." It rarely is.

Most cross-border moves involve:

- Multiple transfers
- Ongoing U.S. income
- Investment repositioning
- Mortgage down payments
- Retirement distributions
- Future inheritance flows

Each conversion repeats the same hidden cost unless addressed deliberately.

Over time, what looks like a few percent becomes tens of thousands of dollars.

THE DIFFERENCE SPECIALISTS MAKE

When Emily's advisor reviewed the transfer, the solution wasn't complicated—it was simply unfamiliar.

Cross-border currency specialists typically offer:

- Transparent exchange rates
- Spreads closer to 0.20%–1.00%
- No embedded bank margin
- Better timing control
- Documentation suitable for tax reporting

On Emily's transfer alone, the difference would have saved more than $1,000.

Multiply that over a lifetime of cross-border movement, and the cost of not knowing becomes obvious.

WHY BANKS DON'T WARN YOU

Banks aren't required to explain spreads in plain language. They aren't incentivized to offer alternatives.

And they assume most clients won't ask.

Nothing about Emily's transfer was improper. Nothing was illegal.

Nothing was "wrong."

It was simply optimized for the bank—not for her.

THE PSYCHOLOGICAL TRAP

Currency loss feels different than other financial mistakes.

There's no bad decision to point to. No market crash to blame.

No risky investment to regret.

Just a quiet realization:

"I should have known—but didn't." That's why this trap is so common.

THE BIGGER LESSON

Currency isn't just a transaction when you live cross-border. It's a strategy.

Handled casually, it erodes wealth invisibly.

Handled intentionally, it becomes a powerful planning tool.

In the next section, we'll look at how Emily rebuilt something she thought she had lost forever: a Canadian credit profile—and how long it actually takes.

BUILDING CANADIAN CREDIT — THE FIRST 12 MONTHS THAT DEFINE EVERYTHING

The first year in Canada is crucial for establishing a solid credit foundation. Without a Canadian credit history, it's essential to focus on these initial steps to build credit responsibly:

1. Apply for a Canadian credit card: Start with a secured credit card if necessary to begin building your Canadian credit profile.
2. Use credit regularly: Make small purchases on your credit card and pay off the balance promptly to demonstrate responsible usage.
3. Keep credit utilization low: Avoid using more than 30% of your available credit to maintain a healthy credit score.

4. Monitor your credit: Regularly check your credit report to ensure accuracy and to track your progress.

By focusing on these steps, you'll be able to establish credit quickly and improve your access to loans, mortgages, and other financial products in Canada.

THE REALITY NO ONE EXPLAINS UPFRONT

When Canadians or Americans move countries, they expect at least partial recognition of past responsibility.

That never happens.

Canada does not "discount" your lack of credit because you lived elsewhere.

It does not accept letters.

It does not extrapolate.

It does not infer.

If you have no Canadian credit file, lenders treat you as credit invisible.

Not risky.

Not irresponsible. Just unknown.

And in lending, unknown is often worse than bad.

WHY THIS MATTERS MORE THAN NEWCOMERS EXPECT

Credit affects far more than loans.

In Emily's first year in Canada, her credit profile influenced:

- Whether she could lease a car
- Her mobile phone deposit
- Insurance premiums
- Utility setup
- Rental approvals
- Mortgage prequalification timelines
- Interest rates offered
- Security deposits required

Credit wasn't just about borrowing.

It was about access.

THE RULE MOST PEOPLE LEARN TOO LATE

In Canada, time matters as much as behavior.

You can be perfect—but still ineligible—simply because your file is young.

Most lenders require:

- A minimum number of active tradelines
- A minimum age of credit history
- Consistent monthly reporting
- Demonstrated utilization management

You can't shortcut that.

You can only sequence it correctly.

EMILY'S 12 - MONTH CREDIT-BUILDING ROADMAP

Emily's advisor laid out a plan that looked almost boring. That was the point.

It wasn't aggressive. It wasn't fast.

It was deliberate.

Months 1–3: Establish existence

The goal wasn't optimization—it was visibility.

Emily:

- Opened one Canadian credit card
- Used less than 20% of the limit
- Made weekly payments
- Avoided balance carryovers
- Kept the account active—but quiet

Within 90 days, she generated her first Canadian credit score. Not impressive.

Not powerful.

But real.

That mattered.

Months 4–6: Add depth

With one tradeline reporting cleanly, the next step was diversification.

Emily:

- Added a second card (retailer or low-limit)
- Requested a modest limit increase
- Maintained low utilization across both
- Continued perfect payment history

This stage wasn't about borrowing more.

It was about showing consistency across accounts.

Lenders don't trust one data point. They trust patterns.

Months 7–12: Demonstrate capacity

Only after six months of clean history did Emily consider installment credit.

She added:

- A small car loan or
- A modest line of credit Nothing stretched.

Nothing unnecessary. By month twelve:

- Her utilization dropped below 10%
- Her file showed both revolving and installment credit
- Her payment history was flawless
- Her score stabilized into lender-acceptable ranges

She was no longer invisible.

WHAT MOST NEWCOMERS DO WRONG

Emily's experience was smooth because she avoided the most common mistakes:

- Applying for too much credit too fast Multiple declines damage momentum.

- Closing accounts too early
- Age matters. Even small cards are valuable.
- Maxing limits "just this once"
- Utilization spikes linger longer than expected.
- Ignoring phone plans and utilities These often report—and matter.
- Assuming income substitutes for credit It doesn't.

Canadian lenders trust history, not explanations.

WHY PATIENCE BEATS PERFECTION

This was the hardest emotional adjustment for Emily.

She wasn't struggling financially. She wasn't irresponsible.

She wasn't inexperienced. She was simply new.

And in Canada's credit system, newness requires time. Emily said later:

"I wasn't rebuilding my finances.

I was waiting for Canada to get to know me." That shift in mindset made the process bearable.

THE MILESTONE MOMENT

At month twelve, Emily applied for financing again—this time with confidence.

The response was different. The tone was different.

The questions were different.

She was no longer being assessed as a risk. She was being evaluated as a client.

That's the quiet power of credit done right.

In the next section, we'll look at the emotional moment that almost broke Emily's confidence—and why Canadian banks weren't rejecting her, even when it felt personal.

WHY DON'T CANADIAN BANKS TRUST ME?" — THE MOMENT MOST NEWCOMERS TAKE PERSONALLY

For Emily, the breaking point didn't come at the teller counter. It came weeks later, sitting across from a lender's desk, reviewing what she assumed would be a routine car loan approval.

Her income was strong.

Her employment was stable. Her finances were organized.

Her credit behavior—so far—had been flawless.

The lender listened politely, typed for a moment, then looked up and said the sentence Emily would replay in her head for days:

"We need at least six months of Canadian credit history."

Emily felt embarrassed. Then angry.

Then confused.

"Six months?" she asked. "I've never missed a payment in my life."

The lender nodded.

"I believe you. We just can't see it yet."

THE EMOTIONAL MISUNDERSTANDING

This is the point where many newcomers internalize the experience.

They assume:

- They are being judged
- They are being penalized for moving
- They are being treated as irresponsible
- They are being discriminated against

None of that is true.

Canadian banks are not saying *no* because they don't trust you.

They're saying *not yet* because they don't know you.

HOW CANADIAN LENDERS ACTUALLY THINK

Canadian lending culture is conservative by design. Banks are regulated differently.

Risk tolerance is lower.

Historical data matters more than potential.

From the bank's perspective:

- A U.S. credit file is legally irrelevant
- Income without history is incomplete
- Newcomers represent unknown behavior patterns
- Time in the system reduces uncertainty

The decision isn't personal. It's procedural.

But when you're sitting across the desk, it doesn't feel that way.

WHY EXPLANATIONS DON'T HELP

Emily did what almost everyone does in that moment.

She explained.

She talked about:

- Her U.S. credit score
- Her perfect payment history
- Her decade of employment
- Her financial discipline
- Her stability

The lender listened respectfully. And still said no.

Because Canadian credit decisions aren't narrative-based. They're data-based.

There is no field in the underwriting system for:

"But trust me."

THE INVISIBLE WAITING PERIOD

What makes this stage particularly frustrating is that Emily was doing everything right.

She was paying on time.

She was keeping balances low.

She was following every instruction. Yet nothing changed immediately.

This is the part no one warns newcomers about: Credit improvement is delayed feedback.

You behave well today.

The system recognizes it months later.

There is no instant validation.

THE MENTAL SHIFT THAT CHANGES EVERYTHING

Emily's advisor reframed the situation in a way that finally made

it bearable.

He said:

"Canada doesn't mistrust you. Canada just hasn't met you yet."

That sentence changed everything.

Instead of feeling rejected, Emily began to see the process as introductions over time.

Every statement. Every payment.

Every month of activity.

All of it was slowly telling her story.

WHY RUSHING BACKFIRES HERE

This is where many newcomers sabotage themselves. Out of frustration, they:

- Apply again too soon
- Add unnecessary credit inquiries

- Accept poor loan terms "just to prove a point"
- Carry balances longer than needed
- Close accounts emotionally

Each of those choices slows progress. Emily didn't rush.

She waited.

She let the system catch up.

THE QUIET TURNING POINT

The shift didn't announce itself.

There was no notification. No congratulatory message.

One day, a pre-approval appeared. Then another.

Then better terms.

The same banks.

The same institutions. Different posture.

That's how Canadian trust works.

It doesn't flip.

It accumulates.

THE LESSON MOST PEOPLE LEARN TOO LATE

Credit in Canada is not about proving worth.

It's about demonstrating predictability over time.

Once Emily understood that, the frustration lost its edge.

She wasn't being rejected.

She was being introduced.

In the next—and final—section of this chapter, we'll look at the one tool that ties everything together: the professional who understands both systems and prevents years of unnecessary mistakes.

THE MOST IMPORTANT CROSS-BORDER TOOL — WHY EVERYTHING FINALLY STARTED TO MAKE SENSE

By the time Emily reached this point, she wasn't confused anymore.

She was tired.

Tired of translating her life between two systems. Tired of being told "that's not how it works here."

Tired of learning rules only after they had already cost her time, money, or peace of mind.

She wasn't reckless.

She wasn't disorganized. She wasn't naïve.

She was simply trying to live in a system that could only see half of her life at a time.

That's when her advisor introduced the concept that quietly resolves more cross-border problems than anything else in this book:

A dual-licensed cross-border advisor.

WHY MOST PROFESSIONALS CAN ONLY SEE HALF THE PICTURE

Up to this point, Emily had interacted with:

- A Canadian bank
- A U.S. credit card issuer
- A Canadian lender
- A U.S. investment platform
- A Canadian tax preparer
- A U.S. tax preparer

Each one was competent.

Each one was well-intentioned.

Each one gave advice that made sense inside their own system.

And that was the problem.

Because Emily's life no longer lived in one system. It lived between them.

A Canadian advisor could not legally advise on U.S. accounts. A U.S. advisor could not legally advise Canadian residents. Banks could open accounts but not coordinate strategy. Accountants could file returns but not design structure.

Everyone was correct.

No one was comprehensive.

THE COST OF FRAGMENTED ADVICE

Before working with a cross-border advisor, Emily's financial life looked like this:

- U.S. accounts reacting defensively to her address change
- Canadian banks treating her as a brand-new entrant
- Currency decisions made transaction by transaction
- Credit strategy happening by trial and error
- Tax residency flipping faster than planning could follow
- Long-term decisions being made under short-term pressure

Nothing was technically "wrong."

But nothing was connected.

That fragmentation is where most cross-border damage happens—not from bad decisions, but from uncoordinated ones.

WHAT " DUAL- LICENSED" ACTUALLY MEANS

A true cross-border advisor isn't just someone familiar with both countries.

They are:

- Licensed to advise under U.S. securities regulation
- Licensed to advise under Canadian regulation
- Authorized to manage accounts on both sides
- Fluent in IRS and CRA coordination
- Experienced in FX strategy, not just conversion

- Able to see timing, sequencing, and consequences across borders

This matters because legality matters.

Advice that cannot be implemented is not advice. It's information.

WHAT CHANGED WHEN EVERYTHING CAME UNDER ONE ROOF

Once Emily's financial life was coordinated through a dual-licensed advisor, several things happened quickly—but not magically.

First, her U.S. accounts stopped reacting defensively. They were restructured into compliant platforms that allowed continued management without triggering freezes.

Second, her Canadian credit strategy became intentional. Instead of guessing, each step was sequenced:

- When to apply
- What to apply for
- What to delay
- What not to touch

Third, currency stopped being an accident.
USD wasn't converted "when needed."
It was managed as exposure, timed, and optimized.

Fourth, tax decisions stopped happening in isolation. Investment structure, credit behavior, and residency were aligned—so one decision didn't undo another six months later.

Emily described it this way:

"For the first time since moving, my financial life felt like one story again — not two arguments happening at once."

WHY THIS ROLE MATTERS MORE THAN EVER

Cross-border living used to be rare.

Now it's normal.

First, her U.S. accounts stopped reacting defensively. They were restructured into compliant platforms that allowed continued management without triggering freezes.

Second, her Canadian credit strategy became intentional. Instead of guessing, each step was sequenced:

- When to apply
- What to apply for
- What to delay
- What not to touch

Third, currency stopped being an accident. USD wasn't converted "when needed."

It was managed as exposure, timed, and optimized.

Fourth, tax decisions stopped happening in isolation. Investment structure, credit behavior, and residency were aligned—so one decision didn't undo another six months later.

Emily described it this way:

"For the first time since moving, my financial life felt like one story again — not two arguments happening at once."

WHY THIS ROLE MATTERS MORE THAN EVER

Cross-border living used to be rare. Now it's normal.

Remote work.

Dual citizenship.

International families.

Split retirements.

Binational estates.

But regulation hasn't caught up.

Systems are still national.

Lives are not.

That gap is where confusion, penalties, freezes, and lost opportunities live.

And it's exactly the gap a cross-border advisor exists to bridge.

THE REAL VALUE ISN'T SOPHISTICATION — IT'S PREVENTION

The true value of cross-border financial planning lies not in sophisticated strategies, but in preventing mistakes. Many financial issues that arise during a move from the U.S. to Canada can be avoided with proactive planning.

Key points:

- Preventive measures like early tax planning and healthcare coordination can prevent costly issues down the road.
- A dual-licensed cross-border advisor ensures that your U.S. and Canadian financial systems work together, avoiding conflicts and inefficiencies.
- It's not about using complex strategies; it's about staying ahead of potential issues before they arise.

By focusing on prevention, you can avoid unnecessary account freezes, tax penalties, and financial missteps, ensuring a smoother transition.

THE QUIET ENDING TO A LOUD CHAPTER

This chapter wraps up with a simple but crucial message: planning is the key to navigating a cross-border move. While the process may seem daunting, most challenges can be avoided with early action and coordinated financial planning.

Key takeaways:

- Proactive planning prevents issues related to credit building, tax residency, and financial integration.

- The importance of working with cross-border advisors to ensure your U.S. and Canadian financial systems are aligned.
- Timely decisions and early preparation are crucial to avoiding financial missteps and ensuring a smoother transition.

A well-prepared approach ensures that the move, although challenging, can be managed efficiently, making it easier to settle into your new life in Canada.

CHAPTER 10
WHEN ESTATE PLANNING CROSSES THE BORDER: WHY "GOOD INTENTIONS" CAN CREATE BAD OUTCOMES

In This Chapter, You Will Learn...

In this chapter, you will learn why estate planning becomes far more complex when assets, family members, or intentions cross the Canada–U.S. border—and how well-meaning plans can unravel without coordination.

Specifically, this chapter explains:

- Why U.S. estate tax can apply to Canadians who are neither U.S. citizens nor residents
- How low U.S. estate and gift tax exemptions for non-residents create unexpected exposure
- What qualifies as U.S.-situs property, and why many families underestimate what's included
- How the Canada–U.S. Tax Treaty works—and why it provides no protection unless filings are made
- Why probate often occurs in multiple jurisdictions and how that delays distributions
- When trusts and holding structures help—and when they make things worse if misused
- How U.S. gift tax rules can penalize simple transfers made with good intentions
- How Canada's deemed disposition on death collides with U.S. estate and state taxes
- Why executors face frozen accounts, IRS liens, and long clearance timelines

- How mixed-citizenship couples are uniquely exposed without proper trust planning
- Why estate planning must be coordinated with tax, immigration, and asset structure—before death, not after

This chapter shows why cross-border estate planning is not about complexity, but about visibility—and why seeing both sides of the border at once is the only way to protect families from avoidable outcomes.

INTRODUCTION — "WE DID EVERYTHING RIGHT... OR SO WE THOUGHT"

Cross-border estate planning failures rarely come from recklessness. They come from reasonable people assuming that good intentions, competent advisors, and signed documents are enough.

They aren't.

This chapter grew out of conversations with professionals who have spent decades watching families do "everything right" inside one country—only to discover that estate planning rules do not stop at the border. A Canadian will does not override

U.S. tax law. A U.S. trust does not automatically align with Canadian tax treatment. And advice that works perfectly in one jurisdiction can quietly create exposure in another.

What makes cross-border estate issues especially painful is when they appear. These problems don't surface during planning meetings. They surface after death—when timelines are compressed, assets are frozen, and families are grieving.

At that point, even simple questions become complicated:

- Why is an estate tax return required if no tax is owed?
- Why can't U.S. property be sold yet?
- Why are accounts frozen?
- Why does the executor need court approval in two countries?

This chapter exists to answer those questions before families are forced to live them.

Cross-border estate planning is not about complexity for its own sake. It is about visibility—understanding how two systems interact, where they collide, and where silence creates risk.

Good intentions are not the problem. Uncoordinated systems are.

ISSUE 1 — U.S. ESTATE TAX EXPOSURE FOR CANADIANS

Canadians who own U.S. assets are often unaware of their estate tax exposure to the U.S. This tax applies to U.S. assets over a certain threshold and can affect individuals even after they leave the U.S. or become Canadian residents.

Key points:

- U.S. estate tax applies to U.S.-situs assets, such as real property or U.S. stocks, above $60,000 for non-U.S. citizens.
- The U.S. estate tax exemption is significantly lower for non-U.S. citizens who are not residents of the U.S. compared to U.S. citizens, leading to potential tax liabilities on the transfer of U.S. assets upon death.
- Tax treaties and strategic estate planning can help mitigate this exposure, but early planning is essential to avoid hefty tax bills.

ISSUE 2 — U.S. ESTATE TAX THRESHOLDS FOR NON-U.S. CITIZENS

Non-resident Canadians who are not U.S. citizens are subject to U.S. estate tax on U.S.-situs assets, such as real estate and stocks, above a threshold of $60,000.

Key points:

- $60,000 exemption: This is the estate tax exemption for non-U.S. citizens, which is significantly lower than the exemption for U.S. citizens ($15 millionas of 2026).
- U.S. estate tax applies to the value of U.S. assets at the time of death, and any assets exceeding the threshold will be taxed at rates ranging from 18% to 40%.
- Tax treaties: The Canada-U.S. tax treaty provides relief in certain situations but doesn't fully eliminate the estate tax liability for non-residents.

Proper estate planning and understanding of U.S. estate tax rules can minimize exposure and prevent unintended tax consequences for heirs.

ISSUE 3 — IDENTIFYING U.S.-SITUS ASSETS

U.S.-situs assets are those located in the U.S. or subject to U.S. law. For Canadians, these assets can trigger U.S. estate tax liabilities, even if they are no longer U.S. residents.

Key U.S.-situs assets include:

- U.S. real estate: Property located in the U.S. is always considered a U.S.-situs asset.
- U.S. stocks and bonds: Even if held in Canadian accounts, investments in U.S. corporations are subject to U.S. estate tax.
- U.S. retirement accounts: 401(k)s, IRAs, and other U.S.-based retirement accounts are also subject to U.S. estate tax.

Understanding these assets and planning for their potential tax implications is essential for minimizing exposure to U.S. estate tax.

ISSUE 4 — USING THE CANADA–U.S. TAX TREATY PROPERLY

The Canada-U.S. Tax Treaty provides important tax relief for Canadians with U.S.-situs assets. However, it's essential to understand how to use the treaty correctly to avoid double taxation.

Key points:

- Estate tax relief: The treaty helps reduce U.S. estate tax exposure by allowing Canadians to claim a unified credit based on the proportion of value of their U.S. assets relative to the value of their worldwide assets. Additional credits for U.S. assets are also available such as the marital credit as well as foreign tax credits for any Canadian estate tax paid.
- Tax treaty elections: Canadians must file specific forms to claim elections (like Form 706-NA for estate tax and Form 8833 Treaty Disclosure) to benefit from the treaty's provisions.
- Cross-border planning: While the treaty provides relief, it may not completely eliminate U.S. estate tax obligations for non-residents, so careful planning is still needed.

By using the Canada-U.S. Tax Treaty properly, Canadians can minimize U.S. estate tax exposure and ensure that their assets pass to heirs without excessive tax burdens.

ISSUE 5 — PROBATE IN MULTIPLE JURISDICTIONS

When dealing with U.S. and Canadian assets, probate can become a complex process. Multiple jurisdictions mean that assets in each country must undergo probate separately, which can lead to delays and increased costs.

Key points:

- U.S. probate: For U.S.-situs assets, U.S. probate laws apply, requiring the appointment of an executor and court oversight.

- Canadian probate: Similarly, Canadian assets are subject to Canadian probate, which can take time, especially if the estate involves both U.S. and Canadian assets.
- Coordination of probate processes: Executors must ensure that the estate is processed in both countries, which can involve additional filings and court procedures.

Proper estate planning, including the use of trusts or wills that address both U.S. and Canadian assets, can simplify this process and reduce costs.

ISSUE 6 — TRUSTS AND HOLDING STRUCTURES

Trusts and holding structures can be effective tools for managing cross-border estates, but they require careful planning to avoid U.S. estate tax and ensure compliance with both U.S. and Canadian laws.

Key points:

- U.S. estate tax exposure: U.S. trusts and holding companies are popular tax planning tools but can potentially still be subject to U.S. estate tax It's crucial to structure them properly to minimize tax exposure.
- Canadian tax considerations: While Canadian tax rules on trusts and holding structures are different from those in the U.S., they can still be effective tools for managing assets. However, they must be structured in a way that does not trigger unwanted income taxes as well as U.S. estate tax.
- Proper structuring: Effective use of intervivos trusts, testamentary trusts, and holding companies requires both tax expertise and knowledge of cross-border laws to avoid creating unintended tax liabilities.

Careful planning of trusts and holding structures ensures that you can preserve wealth across borders while taking into account the tax residency of trustees or executors, to avoid creating unintended cross-border tax obligations.

ISSUE 7 — U.S. GIFT TAX RULES: THE SILENT TRAP

Many Canadians don't realize that U.S. gift tax rules apply to U.S.-situs assets—even if they're living in Canada. These taxes can catch people off guard, especially when gifting assets like U.S. real estate or stocks.

Key points:

- Gift tax exposure: U.S. gift tax applies to gifts of U.S.-situs assets over $19,000 per recipient per year. If you exceed this amount, you could be subject to U.S. gift tax rates.
- Planning ahead: It's essential to understand gift tax implications before making large transfers of U.S. assets.
- Cross-border planning with the right legal and tax advice can help mitigate these risks.

Understanding U.S. gift tax rules and how they apply to Canadians can help prevent unexpected costs during estate planning.

ISSUE 8 — CANADIAN TAX ON DEATH: THE DEEMED DISPOSITION COLLISION

In Canada, when a person passes away, their assets are deemed disposed of at fair market value, which can trigger capital gains tax on U.S.-situs assets.

Key points:

- Deemed disposition: Upon death, Canadian tax rules treat assets as if they were sold at their market value, leading to potential capital gains taxes.
- U.S.-situs assets: This applies to U.S. real estate and stocks. If these assets have appreciated in value, Canadian taxes will be due, even if the U.S. estate tax has already been paid.
- Tax planning: Proper estate planning can help mitigate the impact of deemed disposition, especially when U.S. assets are involved, ensuring that both U.S. and Canadian taxes are efficiently handled.

Understanding how Canadian tax on death intersects with the

U.S. estate tax system is crucial to minimizing the tax burden on your estate.

ISSUE 9 — U.S. STATE ESTATE AND PROBATE RULES

In addition to federal estate tax, U.S. state-level estate taxes and probate rules can significantly impact cross-border estates. Each state has its own set of rules that may complicate the estate process for non-residents.

Key points:

- State estate taxes: Some U.S. states impose their own estate tax, which can be triggered even if the federal estate tax exemption is met.
- Probate processes: The probate process for U.S. assets must comply with state law, and it varies from state to state, adding complexity for Canadian residents with U.S.-situs assets.
- Cross-border planning: Understanding state-specific rules is critical for Canadians with U.S. assets, as these can result in unexpected costs and delays.

Effective planning with cross-border tax advisors can help mitigate state-level estate tax and streamline the probate process.

ISSUE 10 — CROSS-BORDER REPORTING AND COMPLIANCE FAILURES

The most common failure in cross-border estates is not tax—it is paperwork.

Even when no tax is ultimately owed, missing or late filings can result in:

- Frozen bank and brokerage accounts
- Delayed probate and title transfers
- IRS liens on U.S. property
- Inability to sell or refinance assets

U.S. institutions often require proof of tax compliance before releasing assets. This includes filings that many families do not realize are mandatory, such as **estate tax returns filed to claim treaty relief** and the **IRS tax transfer certificate** required for certain retirement accounts, including IRAs. Both documents are common reasons assets may be temporarily frozen until compliance is verified. Once accounts are frozen, families lose control. Bills still need to be paid. Properties still need maintenance. Beneficiaries still need distributions.

The damage here is not theoretical. It is practical, stressful, and time-consuming—and almost always avoidable with coordinated planning before death.

PART TWO — ISSUE 1 — U.S. Probate for U.S. Assets: Why Canadian Wills Aren't Enough

A Canadian will does not control U.S. assets.

That reality catches families off guard more than any tax rule. The Jurisdiction Problem

U.S. assets — especially real estate — are governed by:

- U.S. state probate courts
- State-specific succession rules
- Local procedural requirements

Even with a valid Canadian will:

- U.S. probate is usually required
- A local court filing is mandatory
- Executors may need separate authority
- Timelines are driven by U.S. courts, not Canadian ones

What This Means in Practice

Without proper structuring:

- Two probate processes run in parallel
- Legal costs multiply
- Timelines stretch from months into years
- Assets remain inaccessible during court review

Families often discover this only after death — when no corrective planning is possible.

The Planning Lesson

Probate follows property location, not citizenship or intent. If assets cross the border, probate almost always does too.

In the next section, we'll examine how multiple wills can help — and how poorly coordinated wills can make things much worse.

ISSUE 2 — Multiple Wills: When Separation Simplifies — and When It Backfires

Using separate wills for Canadian and U.S. assets is often recommended in cross-border planning. Done correctly, it can significantly reduce probate delays and administrative overlap. Done poorly, it creates conflict, duplication, and litigation risk.

Why Multiple Wills Exist at All

The logic is straightforward:

- A Canadian will governs Canadian assets
- A U.S. will governs U.S.-situs assets
- Each document is probated only where needed
- Executors can act locally without waiting on foreign courts

This structure can save time and money — but only if the wills are drafted to work together.

Where Things Go Wrong

Problems arise when:

- One will unintentionally revokes the other
- Assets are referenced inconsistently
- Executors are unclear on authority
- Residual clauses overlap
- Amendments are made on one side only

In those cases, courts may be forced to interpret intent — a slow and expensive process.

The Core Rule

Multiple wills must be deliberately coordinated, cross-referenced, and reviewed together.

Separate documents do not mean separate strategies.

ISSUE 3 — Executor Authority Across Borders: Who Can Actually Act?

Being named executor in a Canadian will does not automatically grant authority in the United States.

This surprises many families — and stalls estates at the worst possible moment.

The Legal Reality

U.S. institutions and courts typically require:

- Local probate approval
- Formal recognition of executor status
- Court-issued documentation
- Sometimes, a U.S.-based representative

Without this, even routine tasks become impossible.

Common Consequences

When authority isn't recognized:

- Bank accounts remain frozen
- Property cannot be sold or insured
- Brokerage firms refuse instructions
- Tax deadlines approach without access to information

Executors often feel personally responsible — even though the issue is structural, not procedural.

Planning Ahead

Effective cross-border planning anticipates:

- Where authority will be required
- Which courts must be involved
- Whether co-executors are needed
- How delays can be minimized

Executor authority is not about trust. It's about jurisdiction.

In the next section, we'll look at the filing that unlocks almost everything — the U.S. estate tax return, even when no tax is owed.

ISSUE 4 — Filing the U.S. Estate Tax Return for Nonresidents and Non-Citizens of the U.S. (Form 706-NA): The Gatekeeper Filing

One of the most dangerous misconceptions in cross-border estate administration is this:

"If no U.S. estate tax is owed, no U.S. filing is required." That assumption freezes estates.

Why Form 706-NA Matters

For non-U.S. citizens living outside of the U.S. who owned U.S.-situs assets greater than $60,000, Form 706-NA is often required even when the treaty eliminates tax. This filing is how the estate:

- Claims treaty relief
- Establishes exemption eligibility
- Starts the clock toward IRS clearance

Without it, the IRS treats the estate as unresolved.

What Happens If It's Missed

When the return is not filed:

- Treaty protection is unavailable
- Financial institutions refuse to release assets
- Title companies block property transfers
- IRS transfer certificates cannot be issued

Families often discover this only after months of inactivity — when nothing moves and no one explains why.

The Planning Reality

This filing is not optional administration.

It is the key that unlocks the estate, regardless of tax outcome.

ISSUE 5 — Valuation of U.S. Assets: Where Small Errors Cause Long Delays

Valuation sounds technical. In cross-border estates, it's strategic.

U.S. estate filings require precise, defensible fair-market values for all U.S.-situs assets as of the date of death.

Why Valuation Becomes a Bottleneck Problems arise when:

- Appraisals are informal or outdated
- Currency conversion is inconsistent
- Real estate values lack local support
- Investment values don't align with custodial records

Even minor discrepancies can trigger IRS follow-up — and follow-up means delay.

The Cost of Getting It Wrong

Incorrect or unsupported valuations can result in:

- IRS challenges or requests for clarification
- Refiling requirements
- Delayed transfer certificates
- Extended asset freezes

During that time, estates cannot close — and beneficiaries wait. The Practical Rule

Valuation must be:

- Accurate
- Documented
- Consistent across U.S. and Canadian filings

In cross-border estates, valuation isn't about numbers. It's about momentum.

In the next section, we'll examine how Canadian capital gains tax and U.S. estate tax collide — and why coordination determines whether families pay once or twice.

ISSUE 6 — Coordinating Canadian Capital Gains With U.S. Estate Tax

Cross-border estates face two different tax triggers at death:

- Canada: Applies a deemed disposition, taxing unrealized capital gains immediately. This includes RRSPs and RRIFs, which are treated as deemed distributions at death, resulting in income inclusion on the deceased's final Canadian tax return.
- U.S.: Applies estate tax based on the fair market value of assets, but U.S. IRAs and similar retirement accounts are not immediately taxed. Beneficiaries may generally defer tax on distributions for up to 10 years, allowing for continued tax deferral and planning flexibility.

Coordinating the timing and structure of assets across both systems is essential to minimize double taxation and maximize estate efficiency.

When these systems aren't coordinated:

- The same asset can generate tax in both countries
- Timing mismatches reduce foreign tax credit recovery
- Liquidity shortages arise when taxes are due before assets can be accessed

The key risk isn't double taxation by law — it's double taxation by poor sequencing. Proper coordination aligns valuation dates, currency treatment, and filing timelines so credits actually offset tax paid.

Without that alignment, estates often overpay simply because filings didn't speak to each other.

ISSUE 7 — State-Level Estate or Inheritance Taxes: The Overlooked Layer

Avoiding U.S. federal estate tax doesn't always end the story. Several states impose their own:

- Estate taxes
- Inheritance taxes
- Probate-specific filing rules

These taxes apply independently of federal rules and treaty relief may not fully protect against them.

Location matters. The same property held in two different states can produce very different outcomes.

Families are often caught off guard when:

- State filings are required after federal clearance
- Additional tax is due despite "no U.S. estate tax"
- Local probate delays extend timelines further

State-level exposure must be reviewed early — not discovered mid-administration.

ISSUE 8 — Transfer of U.S. Real Property and the IRS Lien

When transferring U.S. real property after death, the IRS lien can complicate matters for Canadian residents. This lien ensures that U.S. estate taxes are paid before the property is transferred to heirs.

Key points:

- IRS lien: The IRS places a lien on U.S. real property to secure the estate tax liability. This can delay property transfers to heirs until tax liabilities are resolved.
- Cross-border complications: The IRS lien complicates property transfer for Canadians, requiring careful coordination between U.S. and Canadian estate laws.
- Planning ahead: To avoid delays and unexpected complications, it's essential to plan the transfer of U.S. property carefully, considering both U.S. tax obligations and Canadian estate law.

Proper planning can ensure that U.S. real property is transferred smoothly without unnecessary tax hurdles or legal obstacles.

ISSUE 9 — Banking & Brokerage Restrictions After Death

After death, U.S. banking and brokerage accounts can face significant restrictions. These restrictions are usually tied to estate processing and the requirement to satisfy U.S. tax obligations before assets are released.

Notably, for U.S. financial accounts held by Canadian residents, an IRS tax transfer certificate is often required. This certificate is a common cause of account freezes and delays, a problem frequently encountered by Raymond James clients in Canada, even for beneficiaries who are Canadian residents. The certificate ensures that the IRS receives proper confirmation of tax compliance before funds are released.

Key points:

- Account freezes: U.S. banks and brokers may freeze accounts upon notification of death, preventing access to funds until the estate is processed.
- Required documentation: Executors may need to provide proof of death, probate court documents, and other legal paperwork to lift restrictions.
- Cross-border complexities: For Canadians, these processes can be more difficult due to the need to navigate both U.S. and Canadian estate laws.

Planning ahead with a cross-border estate advisor ensures smoother management of U.S. accounts and avoids delays in settling the estate.

ISSUE 10 — Executor Reporting Obligations Across Borders

When dealing with cross-border estates, executors must navigate reporting obligations in both the U.S. and Canada. This can lead to complications due to different reporting requirements for U.S.-situs assets and Canadian assets.

Key points:

- U.S. reporting: Executors must file U.S. tax forms (such as Form 706-NA) for U.S. assets, ensuring compliance with U.S. estate tax regulations.

- Canadian reporting: In Canada, executors need to report all foreign assets, including U.S. real estate and investments, on the Canadian tax return.
- Coordination required: Executors must coordinate tax filings and asset reporting across both jurisdictions to avoid delayed probate and penalties.

Effective planning and early engagement with cross-border advisors ensure proper compliance and smooth administration of the estate.

KEY CROSS-BORDER TRUTHS FROM THE TABLE

The lunch conversations that shaped this chapter revealed a consistent reality:

- The U.S. imposes four transfer taxes: income, estate, gift, and generation-skipping.
- Canada relies on income tax via deemed disposition upon death.

These systems:

- Are not intuitive.
- Do not align automatically.
- Do not forgive missed filings.

Most failures don't stem from aggressive planning. They arise from assuming rules stop at the border.

They don't.

SPECIAL NOTE — MIXED CITIZENSHIP COUPLES

When one spouse is Canadian and the other is a U.S. citizen, estate planning risks increase significantly. A common assumption is that leaving assets outright to a surviving spouse is always safe. However, in cross-border cases, that may not be true.

Key issues include:

- Canadian assets becoming exposed to U.S. estate tax.
- Loss of marital deferral protections for U.S. citizens.

- Unintended inclusion of Canadian wealth in the U.S. taxable estate.

Proper planning involves:

- Carefully structured spousal trusts.
- Coordinated beneficiary designations.
- Explicit treaty-based strategies.

When done correctly, these tools preserve spousal security without creating unnecessary tax exposure. When done casually, they lead to tax outcomes no one intended.

THE RETIREMENT ACCOUNT MYTH

Being named a beneficiary of a U.S. retirement account does not guarantee timely access to the funds after death. Even when there is no estate tax liability, the process can be delayed due to required IRS transfer certificates.

Key issues:

- Account freezes: U.S. retirement accounts are frequently frozen at death, preventing beneficiaries from accessing funds immediately.
- IRS Transfer Certificates: These certificates are often required before funds can be released, leading to delays of up to two years.
- Cash-flow strain: During the freeze, distributions may still accrue, but withdrawals are not permitted, causing financial strain for beneficiaries.

Even for spouses or seemingly simple accounts, the process can be far more complicated than expected.

CONCLUSION — ESTATE PLANNING DOESN'T END AT THE BORDER

Every failure discussed in this chapter shares one trait: Good intentions without cross-border visibility.

Families often have:

- Advisors,
- Wills,

- Trusts,
- Clear wishes.

What they lack is coordination between systems that do not speak to each other.

Canada and the U.S. approach death differently. They tax differently. They administer estates differently. They enforce compliance differently.

Estate planning across borders is not about complexity—it is about alignment.

This chapter exists to help families avoid learning these lessons:

- In probate court,
- On a frozen account screen,
- Or while waiting for clearance that could have been avoided.

The border changes the rules. Planning must change with it.

ABOUT THE AUTHOR

Gerald Scott is the host of the Snowbirds Expat Radio Podcast and creator of the Canada Physical Presence Tracker and Snowbirds U.S. Day Tracker apps.

With over 35 years of experience in the financial services industry, Gerald is a cross-border portfolio manager working with a major North American firm. Through his work with clients navigating life between Canada and the United States, he brings real-world insight, practical strategies, and case-based experience to complex cross-border decisions.

This book is a trusted resource for:

- Canadians returning home after years abroad
- Snowbirds considering a permanent move back to Canada
- Americans relocating to Canada for the first time

A practical, must-have guide for anyone navigating the financial and logistical realities of moving between the U.S. and Canada.

www.ingramcontent.com/pod-product-compliance
Lightning Source LLC
LaVergne TN
LVHW050302210926
848481LV00014BA/590